GREAT SPEECHES
Volume I
SECOND EDITION

Lloyd E. Rohler

Roger Cook

greenwood, indiana

GREAT SPEECHES
Volume I

SECOND EDITION

Copyright 1986 by Great Speeches, Inc., Greenwood, Indiana. All rights reserved. No part of this book may be reproduced in any form, by mimeograph or any other means, without permission in writing from the publisher.

ISBN number 0-9616489-0-2

Printed in the United States of America

To J. Jeffery Auer, Robert Gunderson and Raymond G. Smith: friends, scholars, teachers.

PREFACE

These essays were written to accompany the video tape, "Great Speeches, Volume I." The purpose of the essays is to aid the student in understanding the rhetorical principles underlying the composition and delivery of each speech. Since this is the first in a projected series of volumes, the editors asked each critic to utilize the classical or neo-Aristotelian method in analyzing each speech. The justification for this approach is quite simple. The classical system is the starting point for all discussion of later rhetorical ideas. Students need a thorough grounding in the basics before advancing to other critical approaches.

This book introduces the student to the basic concepts of the classical system through an introductory chapter. Next, five essays demonstrate the usefulness of the classical system in criticizing and explicating contemporary speeches. A concluding chapter highlights those concepts that are most useful to student speakers composing and delivering their own speeches. The book is designed for any course in which speeches are studied and analyzed. Future volumes in the series will extend the range of speakers and critical approaches.

A project such as this could not be accomplished without the help of many people. We have acknowledged a few in the credits of the video production. There remain those who contributed greatly to this book. A special thanks to: Michelle Foote, Diana Rohler and Dianna Stumph for their hours spent behind typewriters; Susan Cook and Loyneta Rhorer for reviewing our work; and, of course, those who contributed their talents to the various essays appearing herein. We also wish to thank the outstanding instructors who became our role models in the study of speech and communication. In addition to those three to whom we dedicate this work, we also acknowledge Dr. Gail Compton of Eastern Michigan University, Dr. Dennis Gouran of Pennsylvania State University and Dr. James Andrews of Indiana University.

Lloyd E. Rohler
Roger Cook

CONTENTS

INTRODUCTION: A CRITICAL SYSTEM   1

JOHN F. KENNEDY'S INAUGURAL ADDRESS 11
   Critic: Nicholas M. Cripe

MARTIN LUTHER KING, JR'S.
"I HAVE A DREAM" SPEECH 29
   Critic: Lloyd E. Rohler

DOUGLAS MACARTHUR'S FAREWELL ADDRESS . . 41
   Critic: Richard Jensen

ADOLPH HITLER'S SPEECH AT
THE NUREMBERG CONGRESS 56
   Critics: Lloyd E. Rohler & J. Justin Gustainis

FRANKLIN D. ROOSEVELT'S
1942 STATE-OF-THE-UNION ADDRESS 68
   Critics: Kurt W. Ritter & Lloyd E. Rohler

A CLOSING WORD TO THE STUDENT 81

APPENDIX: COMPLETE TEXTS
   Inaugural Address: John F. Kennedy 88
   I Have A Dream: Martin Luther King, Jr. 92
   Farewell Address: Douglas MacArthur 97
   Closing Address to the 1934 Nazi Congress
      in Nuremberg: Adolph Hiter 106
   State-of-the Union Address (1942):
   Franklin D. Roosevelt 108

INTRODUCTION: A Critical System

When we watch a movie, listen to a record, or view a new video, we are frequently moved to say, "I like that!" This response describes the feelings or moods aroused by an artistic production. Such a response serves as the basis for a critical evaluation but it is only the beginning. It is impressionistic and when conveyed to others tells them how we feel but not why we do so. If someone else has a different feeling and we wish to understand why we have different views, each of us must go beyond mere statements of preference and give good reasons to support our own viewpoints. We have now moved to the next level of criticism — a rational explanation for our response to a work of art. Even at this level a discussion may not proceed very far unless both observers can find a common vocabulary to describe their responses. This is the value of a clearly defined critical system constructed of orderly procedures: it allows us to compare our responses to the same work of art and to be as clear as possible about our reasons for making a critical judgment. We may still disagree but both of us will find it easier to understand our differences and to be specific about areas of agreement and disagreement.

Because public speaking played such an important role in the oral societies of Ancient Greece and Rome, these cultures developed a system of criticism that has proved useful for over two thousand years. Through the contributions of philosophers such as Plato and Aristotle, and rhetoricians such as Isocrates, Cicero, and Quintilian, a systematic approach to the study, practice, teaching, and criticism of public speaking evolved. This classical system was message-centered and focused on the means by which a speaker could utilize the resources at his disposal to construct a speech to influence a particular audience. To describe this process the Greeks used the word "rhetoric" meaning "the art of persuasion." This book is designed to introduce you to this critical system through an initial discussion of its main features followed by five essays that utilize the classical approach to evaluate a few of the great speeches from the last half century. When you see each of these speeches on the companion Great Speeches video cassette, you can employ the system for your personal critical assessment.

Classical rhetoricians identified four elements in the speech situation that interact: the speaker, the speech, the audience, and the occasion. Each element contributes to the overall effectiveness of the speech in its own right, but the interaction of the elements can be crucial to the success or failure of the speech. The personal characteristics of the speaker as projected through his delivery and self-presentation to the audience are vital. Great speakers are able to convey to the audience a sense of the person behind the message — a meaning that resides not in the mere text but in the life of the speaker himself.

The audience brings to the speech situation its own expectations, experiences, and values. Often the audience's emotions have been aroused before the speaker begins. Sometimes the audience has had the experience of listening to the speaker before. The audience is aware of certain stylistic preferences or idiosyncratic behaviors and anticipates them. When achieved, the symbolic union of the speaker and the audience at a moment in time is the unique characteristic of a public speech.

The speaker has a text (message) to deliver. In some cases the speaker actually wrote the speech. More commonly, the basic text was written by others and the speaker edited it to conform to his personal style. Whether he wrote the entire text or merely parts of it, the speech text is the speaker's responsibility. He will have to answer for the accuracy of its details, the truth of its charges, and the meaning of its message. What the speaker says is important. The reasons he gives to justify policies or actions will be scrutinized by others. Often a speech that is delivered to a favorable audience will be read much more critically by another. Confronted with multiple audiences and critical interpretations by the news media, a contemporary speaker must weigh the relative importance of each to his goal as a speaker and address each, according to his priorities, in the text of his address.

Lastly, the occasion will influence the speaker's reception, the text of the speech, and the audience's expectations. A ceremonial occasion such as Inauguration Day with its high drama of state and its rich tradition of solemn ceremony will heighten the patriotic feelings of the audience and make it more receptive to the speech of the newly elected President. Similarly, the solemnity of the occasion will influence the text of the speech and the demeanor of the speaker.

Although as critics we often focus attention on one or more of these elements in the speech situation to explain the success or failure of a speech, we must not forget that the speech situation is dynamic. All of these elements interact and contribute something to the total success or failure of the speech.

For convenience in teaching rhetoric to their pupils, classical rhetoricians divided the subject into five parts: invention, arrangement, style, delivery, and memory. Each division was an important component in the process of composing and presenting a speech. Briefly, each will be described and then discussed in greater detail.

The process of invention is the preliminary effort of analysis and research to which the speaker must attend before he is prepared to speak on a topic. Next comes arrangement. Once the speaker has found the information, he must consider the proper form for its presentation. The ideas, information, and appeals must be arranged in a format that will engage the audience's attention and be acceptable to them. The third division is style which means appropriate word choice. To be effective a speech must be understood by the audience. Complex ideas must be expressed as clearly as possible. Having composed the speech, the speaker must rehearse its delivery while committing the speech to memory. Delivery emphasizes the speaking skills of the speaker — the combination of voice and physical action that makes the text of the speech come alive for the audience. Memory includes not only techniques for memorizing the speech but the storehouse of knowledge that the speaker can call upon when needed.

Invention refers to the speaker's use of the resources at his disposal. These involve the three forms of proof: ethos, the speaker's reputation or personal credibility, logos, the rational arguments and evidence that the speaker gives to support his claims, and pathos, the psychological or emotional appeals that the speaker makes to the audience. Speakers rarely use one of these forms of proof to the exclusion of the others. The forms of proof are usually combined for total effect. For example, when Martin Luther King claims that black Americans feel like exiles in their own land, he uses his own credibility as a black American who grew up under a segregated social system, combined with specific examples or evidence of segregation in public accommodations and emotional appeals such as patriotic and religious symbols to reinforce his conclusion that segregation is "a shameful condition."

When as critics we examine a speaker's invention, we are concerned with his analysis of the situation and his balanced use of the entire range of proofs available to him to create a speech to influence the audience. Each speaker employs techniques with which he is most comfortable and through which he feels he can accomplish his objectives. For example, Adolph Hitler was a master at using pathos to stir large audiences toward unified action. Generally, emotional appeal by itself has short-lived impact. Critics quickly note a speaker's overreliance on such appeals and question his objectives and sincerity. Similarly, a critic recognizing MacArthur's exclusive reliance on his ethos as a means of proof might question the wisdom of this choice and consider what alternatives were available to him. To a great extent a speaker's use of invention is a key indication of his character, his objectives, and his attitude toward his audience.

Arrangement refers to the order of the ideas in the speech. Critics generally divide arrangement into two categories — the general strategy that the speaker uses in adapting his ideas to the audience and the more specific organizational pattern. Effective speeches have a psychologically compelling order that effectively moves the audience from acceptance of one idea to another. Often great emphasis is placed in the introduction to the securing of good will and the conciliation of any negative feelings so that the audience will follow the speaker's argument. A good example of this strategy is General MacArthur's speech in which his introduction compliments the members of Congress, reminds them of the great patriots who have spoken at the rostrum, and calls for a fair hearing for his ideas. Having secured the goodwill of the audience, MacArthur moves from one idea to another asserting general propositions that the audience will accept until he narrows the focus of the speech to Korea and a justification of his own actions.

Often ceremonial speeches will follow the sequence of past, present, and future in recalling to the audience glorious actions in the past, singling out important aspects of the present, and predicting great accomplishments in the future. This is the pattern of Martin Luther King's speech. He locates the promise of freedom in the sacred writings of the Founding Fathers and the Emancipation Proclamation, notes the failure of the present to make real those promises, and dreams of the glorious day in the future when the promises will come true. Franklin Roosevelt, in his 1942 State-of-the-Union Address, follows a similar sequence when he outlines the despicable actions of the Axis powers, details the sacrifices demanded by the situation, and focuses on the victorious results of our efforts.

The specific organization pattern used by the speaker contributes clarity to the speech. It aids the audience in following the arguments and it indicates the relationship among ideas. Through subordination, it reveals the ideas the speaker considers the most important. Organizational patterns may vary widely from speech to speech depending on purpose and length. All speeches have an introduction, a body and a conclusion. Many include clear thesis statements, and a preview of the organization. Political speeches arguing for or against a specific policy will often include a section anticipating counterarguments and answering them. Ceremonial speeches usually follow the past, present, and future sequence.

A speaker's style is his signature. In combination with delivery, it reveals his sense of who he is and what he is about. The speaker's choice of words involves matters of taste (i.e., sensitivity to that which is appropriate to the situation, and the audience) and knowledge of the language as revealed through the literature of the culture. A speaker's style is not uniform. He must be able to adapt it to the situation and to the needs of the audience. The classical rhetoricians recognized three levels of style — plain, middle, and grand — which correspond to the three purposes of the speaker — to instruct, to delight, and to move or persuade. The plain or natural style is conversational and appropriate to conveying information. The middle style is more metaphorical or philosophical and corresponds to pleasing or delighting an audience. The grand style is vigorous, abundant, or profuse, and is used to persuade. The three levels of style may be used in one speech or a single style may be relied upon exclusively. When a professor lectures to a class, the plain style may be used exclusively. When the same professor speaks to a civic club about a recent trip he and his class made to England, he may use both the plain and middle styles. If the same speaker gives a commencement address, he might rely on the grand style. John Kennedy's Inaugural Address is in the grand style. The word choice, the sentence structure, and the abundant use of metaphors aim for an overwhelming effect on the audience. In contrast, General MacArthur's speech is in the plain style as he informs his audience of the situation in the Pacific.

Delivery may be divided into two parts, physical action and voice, although obviously both combine to make a strong impression on the audience. The use of physical action to convey meaning is the most difficult skill for beginning speakers to develop, and has posed problems for teachers of public speaking as well. The two approaches to the teaching of gestures may be grouped under the headings of natural and artificial. The natural approach relies on the emotional involvement of the speaker in the speech situation to motivate physical activity. If a speaker feels strongly about his message, he will be carried along by his emotions and physically display his concern. The artificial school believes that although this may occur for experienced speakers, beginning speakers will need rehearsal and conscious effort. Four of the five speakers on the tape fall under the influence of the natural school. Only Hitler followed the artificial school and consciously rehearsed his gestures.

Before the development of newsreels, motion pictures, and televison; a speaker needed gestures to project vitality and convey emphasis and meaning to large crowds that could only view the speaker from a distance. With television close-up pictures, a mass audience of millions of individuals can easily see facial expressions involving small movements of the eyes. As a consequence, broad sweeping movements of the arms are not only unnecessary but appear exaggerated. Obviously a speaker's style is greatly influenced by the media of the era. Adolph Hitler was most effective when he appeared in person before mass rallies. Franklin Roosevelt brought his intimate "Fireside Chats" into living rooms throughout the country on radio. John Kennedy seemed a "natural" for television — his subtle smile and direct look into the camera turned his appearances into one-on-one conversations with millions.

Memory is the last division of classical rhetoric and the most neglected today. In an age of teleprompters, speakers need not take the time to memorize their speeches. Elaborate systems of mneumonic devices such as the Ancients used are passé. But memory meant more to the Ancients than the ability to recite a text. It encompassed familiarity with the commonplaces — those lines from poetry, sacred hymns, popular songs, nonsense rhymes, and fables that encompassed the collective wisdom and experience of the culture. In ancient Greece and Rome books were expensive and rare. The education of the young included memorization of long passages of epic poetry, stories of the gods, and exploits of the heroic warriors and leaders of the past. Today's educational system rarely asks the student to memorize even a line from the great literature of our past. What we have lost is well illustrated on the tape of Martin Luther King's speech. The entire "I have a dream" sequence was not a part of King's written text. He completely extemporized the lines — finding them in his memory. He took lines from previous speeches, verses from the Bible, stanzas from patriotic songs and Negro spirituals to make a moving and memorable conclusion. In doing so, he illustrated for the contemporary student the value of memory, i.e., having a storehouse of commonplaces that can be called upon when necessary.

The Greek and Roman rhetoricians noticed that rhetorical forms used by speakers in recurring situations shared certain characteristics. Legal speeches concerned themselves with the issues of justice or injustice and used as primary means tactics of accusation and defense. Epideictic or ceremonial speeches focused on honor and dishonor and utilized praise or blame. Political or deliberative speeches primarily concerned themselves with the advantages or disadvantages of policy choices and used encouragement or warnings to move the audience. These genres or types represent a general tendency; rarely will a speech be a pure example of a type. Identifying the genre of a speech will help to clarify the speaker's duties and will aid in evaluating how well he utilized the persuasiveness of form in satisfying audience expectations.

The classical system outlined above focused on the construction of a persuasive message for a particular audience. It assumed that certain recurring rhetorical forms worked on an audience because they corresponded to the way individuals decided upon the "Truth." The selection of proofs, and their arrangement in a certain format compelled the audience to accept the claims of the speaker because that total effect of the message was satisfying. Given the assumptions of the system, the major criterion for evaluating the success or failure of a speech is audience response. A successful speech satisfies the requirements of the situation and gains audience approval. The critic evaluates the speech against an ideal standard. Did the speaker utilize all the available proofs to achieve the maximum impact on the audience?

The development of the mass media and the multiplication of audiences has modified this criterion for the contemporary critic. Often speeches are staged before a friendly audience but really designed to influence those listening or viewing the speech far removed from the speaker in space and time. Given this situation, the critic must clearly specify the nature of the speaker's "true" audience and the speaker's effectiveness with that audience. Is the speech to be judged by the reactions of the immediate audience or the delayed effect it had on the opinion leaders of the society? Is the critic concerned with the long-term effect of the speech on public opinion as reflected in actual policy choice?

Some of these effects are easier to determine than others. We can count the number of times the immediate audience interrupted the speech with applause and we can see visible reactions of agreement or disagreement on films made of the event. The delayed reaction of the leaders of public opinion can be followed in the editorial columns of the newspapers and journals of opinion in the days following the speech. Sometimes public opinion polls are available to document swings in the public mood following a major speech by a leading political figure. Over an extended period of time, the critic may find recurring references in interviews, speeches, public documents, autobiographical accounts, and scholarly studies to a major speech as the catalyst of change. Even then the critic must be aware of the many factors that influence public opinion and the many pressures that shape policy making and not overestimate the influence of a single speech.

Another way to assess the effectiveness of a speech is to focus on the effect it had on the speaker's overall objectives. The critic can try to understand the speaker's motivation for giving the speech and assess how completely he achieved his purpose. If the speech were designed to gain the nomination for a political office, did the speech help or hinder in the effort? The critic must realize that a speaker may have several goals in mind for a speech and that failure to achieve the primary goal may not make the speech a total failure. A well received speech in a losing cause may be counted a partial success if it brings recognition and marks the speaker as a rising star. How the speech influenced the speaker's reputation may be assessed by examining political commentary and public opinion polls.

If the critic is examining delayed effects, he may notice whether the speech affected the ability of the speaker to act in ways that hindered his career. Sometimes speakers become the victims of their own words. Richard Nixon found that speeches on the growing political scandal in his administration not only failed to gain him public support but limited his freedom of action. Sometimes speakers make predictions or issue warnings that later events prove false. The series of speeches that Charles Lindbergh made against American intervention in Europe prior to the Japanese attack on Pearl Harbor greatly diminished his heroic status.

We can see that the speech critic's task is a complex and frequently uncertain assignment. As you watch the five speeches on the Great Speeches video tape, you should be aware that, although each speaker approached his particular speech in a unique way, dictated by unique events; each speaker also shared some similar characteristics. For each speaker, this was a critical speech — a pivotal moment in his life. Each had, at his disposal, the same resources and methods employed by the Ancient Greeks and Romans to influence an audience. True, they exercised individual choice in selecting those methods which would best serve their purposes, but they nonetheless shopped from the same list.

The ancient Greeks and Romans taught by example. Great or even good examples of public speech are infrequent. We have set out to provide you with a few examples from the recent past. We do not intend for you to attempt to duplicate. A good speaker, however, borrows, adapts, refines and augments the work of others. We have provided five rather diverse examples of a great speech. In each case you will have the opportunity to view the speech, read the text, and study a critical review by a scholar in the field of rhetorical criticism. You should be able to develop your own critical assessment.

John F. Kennedy
Inaugural Address

"Ask not what your country can do for you, ask what you can do for your country."

CRITIC: Nicholas M. Cripe

THE SPEAKER

John Fitzgerald Kennedy's Inaugural Address, ranked by critics among the great inaugural addresses, launched in memorable fashion a Presidency that was to last but a dramatically short thousand days. Kennedy, forty-six years old when assassinated in Dallas, Texas, November 22, 1963, was the youngest man ever elected to the Presidency and the youngest to die in that office.

The first Catholic to be elected President, Kennedy inherited his religious and political party affiliations. His parents were the grandchildren of Irish Catholic immigrants. Joseph Kennedy, his father, graduated from Harvard and became one of the wealthiest men in the United States. An active Democrat, he held several important political appointments including that of Ambassador to Great Britain during FDR's administration. Rose Kennedy was the daughter of John F. (Honey Fitz) Fitzgerald, a wealthy and legendary Boston Democrat politician. John Fitzgerald Kennedy grew up in a family where politics was considered on honorable profession and going to Mass on Sunday morning was an act of faith.

When elected to Congress from a Boston district in 1946, John Kennedy was a cum laude graduate of Harvard and an authentic hero of World War II but, at best, only a fair public speaker. For many years the reporters covering his speeches saw a man who did not enjoy public speaking and was not very good at it. But over the years, and particularly during the 1960 primaries and the Presidential campaign, he successfully worked at improving his delivery. His speaking changed. Theodore Sorenson, Kennedy's principal speech collaborator, tells us:

> *The Congressman and freshman Senator whose private conversations were always informed and articulate but whose public speeches were rarely inspired or inspiring became the candidate and President whose addresses stirred the hearts of the world . . . He became less shy and more poised in his public appearances . . . became in time the President who welcomed every opportunity to get away from his desk and get back to the people.*[1]

From his first campaign for Congress, Kennedy's speeches had been "so uttered as to make him worthy of belief." He was elected to the House of Representatives in three consecutive elections, and in 1952 defeated Senator Henry Cabot Lodge in one of the political upsets of the day. The popular Lodge lost by 70,000 votes in a year when Eisenhower carried the state by an overwhelming majority; Kennedy became only the third Democrat to be elected to the Senate from Massachusetts.

Although reporters may have been critical of Kennedy's delivery, audiences liked him. They responded to the warmth of his smile, his directness, and "his sincerity." Audiences believed him. Time magazine's election edition gave an excellent description of the Kennedy appeal:

> *In appearance he is a slender man with a boyish face, an uncontrollable shock of hair, a dazzling smile. In manner he is alert, incisive, speaking in short, terse, sentences in a chowderish New England accent that he somehow makes attractive . . . reaching with no apparent effort into a first class mind for historical anecdotes or classical allusions . . . he projects a kind of conviction and vigor even when talking of commonplace things in a commonplace way."*[2]

Kennedy's ethos as a speaker played a major role in his becoming President. Through his speaking he gained the public support that led to his election. Kennedy's successful race for the Presidency began with his nominating speech for Adlai Stevenson at the 1956 Democratic National Convention.[3] Kennedy came to the convention interested, available, and frequently mentioned for the vice-presidential nomination, but did not consider himself to be a serious candidate. The night before the Presidential nominations began, Stevenson invited Kennedy to deliver the principal nominating speech. Kennedy accepted and the resulting speech was a success with the convention delegates and the national TV audience. Upon being nominated Stevenson dramatically announced he would leave it to an open convention to select his running mate. The positive response to the nominating speech inspired Kennedy to try for the vice-presidential spot. In the ensuing TV drama played out in the living rooms of America, Kennedy lost the nomination to Estes Kefauver by a handful of votes. In losing he gained more than in winning. Had he won the nomination and been defeated with Stevenson, some political leaders would have blamed the loss on Kennedy's Catholicism, thus possibly ending any hope for a future nomination. As it was, his prominent role in the convention, his speech for Stevenson, his close race with Kefauver, and his graceful acceptance of defeat made him a nationally acclaimed figure. Clearly it was this 1956 convention that first made John Kennedy a leading contender for the 1960 Democratic nomination for President.

Several things combined to make John Kennedy, the candidate and the President, the successful speaker he was. One was his deep confident belief in himself and his abilities to do the job. It was not arrogance but a quiet self-confidence that his audience sensed. When Kennedy declared his intention to seek the Presidency, no one in the upper echelons of the party was for him. Truman and other national party leaders thought he had the wrong religion, the wrong age, the wrong job, and the wrong home state to be nominated and elected President. Many did, however, favor him for the vice-presidency; both to avoid charges for anti-Catholicism, and to bring back to the party the many Catholic Democrats who had voted for Eisenhower. Kennedy did not ignore party leaders nor did he follow their advice. During the three years prior to 1960 he spoke at political meetings around the country, established contacts, gained good will, and cultivated support in those states which held primaries to choose delegates. Consequently, this confident young man went into the primaries with more support among rank and file Democrats than any other candidate.[4]

Another strong ethos factor for Kennedy was his intelligence. Audiences sensed that he knew what he was talking about. Sorenson describes his speeches: "They were generally factual, direct and specific . . . They conveyed a sense of concern and conviction, a vast command of information, a disdain for demagoguery and a mood of cool, decisive leadership."[5] Kennedy trained himself to read rapidly and to retain what he read. He maintained notebooks of quotations, poems, and articles. He utilized these to construct speeches filled with statistics, historical references, and quotations. Audiences perceived him as a well informed, intelligent speaker.

Kennedy's temperament contributed to his ethos. He had an ability to keep his temper and coolness of mind even when provoked. He seldom lost sight of other people's motives and problems. He seemed to instinctively possess the ability to see the situation from their point of view and to react accordingly.

Schlesinger recounts an incident during the 1960 campaign when Kennedy and a group of friends went to a famous New York City restaurant for dinner. At a neighboring table a man, who obviously had been drinking, began to direct unprintable comments to Kennedy. Kennedy's friends raised their own voices hoping to keep him from hearing the comments, but without success. One of his friends started to call the headwaiter; but Kennedy stopped him, saying, "No, don't bother. Think how the fellow's wife must be feeling." His friends looked and saw her flushed with embarrassment.[6]

Not the least of his charm was his wit and sense of humor. Spontaneous and sharp, his wit could silence a heckler while bringing a laugh. During a parade a high school boy yelled at him, "How did you become a hero?" Kennedy's reply brought a cheer, "It was involuntary. They sank my boat." At the Los Angeles Convention a reporter asked Kennedy, "Do you feel, objectively, that a Protestant could be elected President?"

Amid general laughter, a straightfaced Kennedy replied, "If he is prepared to answer questions about the separation of church and state, I see no reason to discriminate against him." The 420 attending reporters gave him a standing ovation.[7]

His confidence, his intelligence, his self-control, his wit, and his sense of humor all combined during those long months of campaigning to create a favorable image in millions of minds. Salinger described the Kennedy ethos:

Eloquence depends not only on the words but on the man, the subject, and the situation. Kennedy was still no orator. Others could be more forceful in voice, gestures, emphasis and pauses. But as Lord Rosebery said of the impassioned oratory of Pitt, it was "the character which breathes through the sentences" that was so impressive. Kennedy's character could be felt in every word . . .[8]

On November 8, 1960, Kennedy won one of the closest Presidential races in our history. In an election in which 64.5% of the eligible voters voted and 68,832,818 Americans cast their ballot for a President, Kennedy carried the Electoral College 303 votes to 219 for Nixon but won the popular vote by only 112,881 votes. In winning Kennedy had the same Electoral College total as Truman in 1948, but got 11 million more votes than Stevenson did in 1956. Kennedy's ethos, the confidence he inspired in his listeners, won him the Presidency. Theodore White in his book, **The Making of the President 1960**, summarizes the election this way: " . . . the election of 1960 was a personal victory for John F. Kennedy, not for his Party."[9]

INAUGURATION DAY: THE OCCASION

January 20, 1961, Inauguration Day, brought sunny, windy, bitter cold weather. Thousands of servicemen worked the previous night and into the morning clearing away eight inches of snow that virtually immobilized Washington. The temperature officially reached 22 degrees when the swearing in ceremony began. Time magazine recounting the occasion said, "Foul weather and a fine speech provided the most memorable moments of a historic week . . . A blizzard threatened to turn the whole momentous occasion into a farce — but President John Kennedy delivering his inaugural address more than saved the day."[10]

Inauguration Day in the United States is the equivalent of an English Coronation, only happening with more frequency and somewhat less pomp. John Kennedy began the day by attending mass. Then he and his wife drove to the White House for coffee with the Eisenhowers, the Lyndon Johnsons, the Richard Nixons and several congressional leaders. Following this congenial social period, President Dwight Eisenhower and President-elect John Kennedy emerged from the White House smiling and in the top hats Kennedy mandated for the platform dignitaries. They stepped into the long black bubble-topped presidential limousine, and drove down Pennsylvania Avenue to Capitol Hill. Along the wide avenues thousands of cheering onlookers greeted them. The bitter cold did not diminish the size nor dim the enthusiasm of the crowds. The fur coats, bright colored stocking caps and blankets added even more color to the occasion.

The ceremony ran behind schedule and John Kennedy's term as President of the United States had run for thirteen minutes according to the Constitution when he stepped out onto the windswept platform and took his seat next to Eisenhower. The platform was filled with the political elite of Washington and the nation: Justices of the Supreme Court, members of the Senate and House Representatives, new Cabinet members, Joint Chiefs of Staff, the diplomatic corps, and families and friends of the chief participants. The plaza in front of the platform was packed with the party faithful anxious to celebrate the change of administrations and to cheer their new leader.

The Marine Band struck up "America the Beautiful" and the ceremonies were underway. Marian Anderson sang "The Star Spangled Banner." As Boston's Cardinal Cushing began what was to be an unduly long invocation, smoke started wafting from the lectern. The Cardinal prayed on and on ignoring the plume of smoke. When he finally closed, Vice President Nixon and several others rushed to the lectern, located the fire in a short-circuited electric motor, and pulled the connecting plug.

The smoke quickly drifted away.

Lyndon Johnson took his oath as Vice-President and clearly muffed a line. Next came one of the most emotional moments of the program. Kennedy had invited Robert Frost to read a poem as part of the ceremony. Frost attempted to read a newly written dedication to his famous poem, "The Gift Outright." Blinded by the bright sun, the wind whipping the paper in his hands, the 86 year old poet faltered, started over, and faltered again. Lyndon Johnson tried to shade the paper with his hat, but it did not help. Frost tried again, stopped, then turned to the microphones and said, "This was supposed to be a preface to a poem that I can say to you without seeing it. The poem goes this way . . ." The nervous titters of the embarrassed crowd stopped as Frost recited from memory in a clear, strong, almost young voice the poem he had chosen for this President.

Despite the biting wind snapping the flags on the platform and surrounding buildings, John Kennedy left his top hat and coat on his chair when he stepped forward to join Chief Justice Earl Warren at the lectern. He took the oath of office which every Chief Executive has sworn to uphold since that April day in 1789 when George Washington became the first President of the United States. Perhaps taking off his top coat was a conscious gesture, perhaps it was not, but it clearly indicated Kennedy's sense of the solemnity of this very special occasion. As his opening words quickly indicated, he was quite conscious of the historical significance of this ceremony.

Having been duly sworn in as President, he turned to face the bank of microphones and the waiting crowd before him. The speech he delivered made this inaugural memorable.

THE SPEECH

A Presidential Inaugural Address is a unique form of public speech which falls under the broad definition of ceremonial speaking. Ceremonial speeches have a variety of forms but a centrality of purpose. Whether the speech is a commencement address, a eulogy, a presentation of an award, or an acceptance speech, it shares the common function of reaffirming and intensifying social values. Scholars identify these speeches this way:

> At moments like these, speakers address audiences about the values that both share as members of a common group. The speeches given in such moments are thus noncontroversial for a specific audience. They do not urge adoption of new values or rejection of old values. Rather they seek to reinforce and revitalize the existing audience values. The speaker seeks unity of spirit or re-energizing of effort or commitment; he tries to inspire, to kindle enthusiasm, or to deepen feelings of awe, respect, and devotion.[11]

Whether it was Lincoln asserting "With malice toward none, with charity for all . . .;" or Franklin Roosevelt telling the American people, "We have nothing to fear, but fear itself;" or John Kennedy asking his fellow citizens to "Ask not what your country can do for you — ask what you can do for your country;" American Presidents have used the inaugural address to appeal to their countrymen to take pride in their country, to cherish her long held traditions, and to put behind them the divisiveness of the past campaign and unite for the common good. From George Washington to the present, Presidents have delivered inaugural addresses which range in distinction from the mundane to the sublime in extolling these values, but few have achieved either the immediate or lasting favorable response to their efforts that John F. Kennedy did for the speech he delivered on January 20, 1961.

Every President hopes his inaugural address will be a memorable one, and John Kennedy was no exception. As The New York Times reported, "President-elect John Kennedy worked today on an inauguration address he obviously wants to make one of the lasting documents of American history . . . Mr. Kennedy has already worked over several drafts of it, it was understood." Kennedy started thinking about the inaugural address in November, for it was shortly after the election that he solicited suggestions from Adlai Stevenson, John Kenneth Galbraith, and others; and suggested to Sorenson he read previous inaugural speeches plus Lincoln's Gettysburg Address. But as Salinger points out, Kennedy was determined from the outset that the speech "would be his and his alone."[12] And it was. Salinger, Sorenson, and scholars agree that this speech was Kennedy's own.

From the organization, wording, and content of the speech it is clear that Kennedy knew that he would be addressing a wide and varied audience. While the speech was clearly intended for the American public, it was also adapted to a world wide audience.

From the beginning of the preparation of this speech, Kennedy wanted to be brief. In fact, until be became aware of the extreme brevity of Roosevelt's Fourth Inaugural Address, he aspired to make his the briefest on record. This concern plus his desire to appeal to more than the domestic audience contributed to his decision to concentrate on foreign policy — a topic in which all his listeners were vitally interested.

The organization of this speech is clear and simple — an introduction that focuses attention and clarifies the topic, a three segment body, and a conclusion that ends the speech on a note of inspiration.

Kennedy opens the speech with the classical techniques of a direct reference to the speaker, the audience, and the occasion. Having established the relation of the present ceremony to the long, solemn tradition of the past, he then quickly brings the traditional meanings to the present, "that the torch has been passed to a new generation of Americans," a generation of Americans believing strongly in their Revolutionary heritage.

Kennedy concludes the introduction by stating the premise of his speech: "Let every nation know, whether it wishes us well or ill, that we shall pay any price, bear any burden, meet any hardship, support any friend, or oppose any foe to assure the survival and the success of liberty. This much we pledge — and more."

The body is divided into three sections. Kennedy first directs his pledges to the various foreign segments of his audience. He begins with "those old allies whose cultural and spiritual origins we share," moves to various other segments of the world, then to the United Nations, "our last best hope." This section has obviously been directed to the friendly and neutral members of his foreign audience.

The second section is directed "to those nations who would

make themselves our adversary." A good example of the attention given to wording in this speech is that the word adversary replaced enemy in the final draft because it had a less hostile connotation. The USSR and her allies are not mentioned by name, but the audience knew to whom the message was addressed. In these two sections the relationship of the ideas is made clear by the parallel structure of the sentences.

In the final section of the body, Kennedy comes back to his American audience, appealing to them to join him in a "struggle against the common enemies of men: tyranny, poverty, disease, and war itself." Only five short paragraphs, this section's clarity comes not from any organizational pattern, but rather from the careful structuring of the language.

Kennedy's conclusion is a textbook example of what a speech conclusion should do. It is short and focuses the audience's thinking on the response desired, while at the same time ending the speech on a note of completeness and finality. The conclusion begins with the unforgettable, "And so my fellow Americans: Ask not what your country can do for you — ask what you can do for your country." He quickly challenges his other audience, the citizens of the world, and then puts the responsibility on both as he ends his speech with words that left no doubt the speech was concluded: "With good conscience our only sure reward, with history the final judge of our deeds, let us go forth to lead the land we love, asking His blessing and His help, but knowing that here on earth God's work must truly be our own."

The simplicity of the organization lies in the fact that the listener is never made aware that there is a pattern. Each succeeding sentence unobtrusively links to the one preceding it. Each paragraph leads naturally into the one following it. Not the least of the values for students of his speech is the recognition of the seemingly artless fashion in which this speech was so artfully formed. This is a speech that literally flows from the opening words to the closing sentence.

In this day of "ghostwriting," two questions students of public address studying a speech must answer are, "How much of this speech is the speaker's?" and "Whose ideas are these; whose language?" In this case the evidence is overwhelming, the language, the ideas, and the speeches he gave were Kennedy's. Of course he had help in the preparation, because no person running for President of the United States or serving as President can find time to prepare by himself all the various speeches demanded. The time has long passed when a Herbert Hoover could literally shut down the Oval Office while he spent days writing a speech. Sorenson and others have frequently pointed out, Kennedy was the architect of the speeches he gave, extemporaneous or manuscript. He was the chief contributor to the planning of strategy and to the securing of supporting materials. Sorenson or some others would frequently then write a first draft, but the final product was Kennedy's.

Salinger tells us: "Actually, speeches were not written for the President but with him. He knew what he wanted to say and how he wanted to say it. The role of the speech writer was to organize JFK's thoughts into a rough draft, on which he himself would put the final touches. His versions would often change it dramatically."[13]

Golden tells us: "When time permitted and the occasion challenged him, Kennedy moved from his typical role of outliner, editor, and collaborator to that of creator. Here he selected his own topic and emphasis, gathered much of his supporting material, then organized and expressed the ideas in hand written manuscripts . . . it was the mode of preparation which Kennedy used in . . . (his) Inaugural Address."[14]

As with Lincoln's Gettysburg Address, it was not so much the ideas as the wording of those ideas that made Kennedy's Inaugural Address memorable. The ideas had been expressed by others before, but never before had they been expressed in such a memorable manner.

One of the distinctive attributes that Lincoln, Roosevelt, Churchill, and Kennedy shared was a sense of style. That is why, when time permitted, their speeches frequently went through so many drafts prior to delivery. Sorenson says of the Inaugural Address, "No Kennedy speech ever underwent so many drafts. Each paragraph was reworded, reworked, and reduced."[15] For example:

First Draft
We celebrate today not a victory of party but a sacrament

of democracy.
Next-to-Last Draft
We celebrate today not a victory of party but a convention of freedom.
Last Draft
We observe today not a victory of party but a celebration of freedom.
First Draft
Each of us, whether we hold office or not, shares the responsibility for guiding the most difficult of all societies along the path of self-discipline and self-government.
Next-to-Last Draft
In your hands, my fellow citizens, more than mine, will be determined the success or failure of our course.
Last Draft
In your hands, my fellow citizens, more than mine, will rest the final success or failure of our course."[16]

Nor, apparently, did Kennedy quit reworking the speech even after the supposed final draft had been released to reporters on the evening of January 19, with the stipulation that it should not be published until after the actual presentation. Reporters had learned to pay attention to such stipulations for a Kennedy speech; many referred to him as "That well known text deviant." They found 30 differences in word choice, sentence structure, and grammatical form in the speech they heard and the copy they had been given. For instance, the reporters' copy read, "Those who foolishly sought to find power by riding on the tiger's back inevitably end up inside." They heard the President say, "Those who foolishly sought power by riding the back of the tiger ended up inside."[17]

Even the antithetical sentence by which this speech is most frequently identified changed. In the reporters' copy, "Ask not what your country will do for you . . . in the speech became "Ask not what your country can do for you . . ."[18]

Kennedy used the "Ask not . . ." expression in prior speeches, but seldom has the importance of wording to the impact of an idea ever been more vividly demonstrated than in this speech. In his Acceptance Speech at the National Democratic Convention, July 15, 1960, Kennedy said, ". . .

the New Frontier of which I speak is not a set of promises — it is a set of challenges. It sums up not what I intend to offer the American people, but what I intend to ask of them." At a Labor Day Rally in Detroit, the phrasing became more audience directed, "The New Frontier is not what I promise I am going to do for you. The New Frontier is what I ask you to do for our country." Finally, in the Inaugural Address, he had in one dramatic sentence focused the attention of the American public on its challenging role in his administration.

Kennedy was no ordinary wordsmith, he was an artisan in working with words. To discuss his craftmanship in detail would be a long essay in itself, but let us notice a few examples. In this speech, Kennedy uses many abstract words, but abstractions to which his audience would respond favorably.

Probably the most notable stylistic quality of this speech is the sentence structure. It is with the structuring of the sentence — the variety of length, the various stylistic devices, the rhythm — that he achieved the emphasis and the impact of this speech.

Kennedy was familiar with many of Lincoln's speeches, particularly his Gettysburg Address. It is quite possible Lincoln's affinity for short sentences and short words influenced the Kennedy style, for these characteristics are to be found frequently in this speech. For example, asyndeton, the stylistic device of omitting the conjunctions between co-ordinate sentence elements, is an effective tool to cut out words and at the same time gain a forceful effect. Kennedy used this device when he said, ". . . we shall pay any price, bear any burden, meet any hardship, support any friend or oppose any foe to assure the survival and the success of liberty." His use of antithesis, repetition in successive clauses in reverse grammatical order, for brevity and emphasis appears in his "Ask not what your country can do for you — ask what you can do for your country." and "Let us never negotiate out of fear. But let us never fear to negotiate."

Kennedy's use of parallelism to give emphasis and forcefulness to his ideas has been mentioned previously. Add the use of contrast, comparison, metaphor, and the rhythm that pervades the entire speech, and it becomes evident why this speech has long been recommended to speech students as an excellent example of "wording the speech." This is a speech that has achieved historical significance not so much because of what Kennedy said, but because of the language with which he said it.

It was only late in the Presidential campaign that Kennedy's voice became a dependable and effective instrument that strengthened rather than weakened response to what he said. As a speaker he was always knowledgeable, sometimes witty, but he possessed a voice that lacked depth and variety, and frequently became high pitched. On several occasions the strain on his throat from constant campaigning left him voiceless and others had to substitute for him. His voice had a definite Harvard-Boston accent. He had a tendency to interject "ers" and "ahs" rather than pauses while speaking at a very rapid rate. At the beginning of the 1960 Presidential campaign, speech teachers who heard him and the reporters who were with him at every speech agreed that he was a poor public speaker.

Kennedy consistently abused his voice during the primaries, losing it entirely for a time in West Virginia, Indiana, and Oregon. He strained it again speaking at the numerous caucuses at the Los Angeles convention so that even a few weeks of rest in the Cape Cod sun did not ease all the soreness. At this time Kennedy, aware of how Wendell Willkie lost his voice in the crucial last days of the 1940 campaign, decided to do something about his vocal delivery.

The New York Times for August 22, 1960 reported: "Senator John F. Kennedy . . . has disclosed to close friends that his occasional loss of voice results from the faulty speech habit of talking from his throat. So, when he can find a free moment from politicking, the Demoractic candidate from Massachusetts is taking lessons on speaking from the diaphragm." A reporter for Time who followed his California swing in middle September, said, "Under the direction of Voice Coach Blair McCloskey, the Kennedy voice was usually well modulated, right from the diaphragm. But occasionally it launched into uncontrolled stridency."

As the campaign was drawing to a close, Douglas Cater writing in The Reporter, October 27, 1960, observed:

Kennedy has come a long way since he first began his

relentless drive for the Presidency. For one thing, with help of coaches he is beginning to master the art of projecting his voice so that it has lost some of its shrill, grating quality . . . There is still an unfinished quality about his oratory. But for brief moments, mainly during the gigantic outside rallies, he has achieved an eloquence that is distinctively his own.

During the fall Presidential campaign Kennedy's vocal delivery noticeably improved. His voice grew less nasal, less harsh and developed more cadence. His Harvard-Boston accent became less pronounced though still noticeable at times. He was learning to pace rather than rush his sentences, thus giving his audiences the opportunity to applaud, to laugh, and to follow and appreciate what he was saying. As his Inaugural Address demonstrates so vividly, Kennedy learned to adapt his delivery as well as his ideas and language to the audience and occasion. His speaking changed for the better because he was willing to recognize weaknesses and take the time and effort to learn how to correct them. Like so many things in life, speaking well in public can be an acquired ability. Kennedy acquired this ability.

However, one aspect of Kennedy's delivery never did change, his limited variety of gestures. Kennedy had two — the pointed finger long jab, and the short jab, usually with the right hand.

The Kennedy Inaugural Address was a well delivered speech, read from a manuscript with excellent eye contact. The overall delivery rate and cadence of the speech adapted well to the solemnity of the occasion. For a speaker notorious for rushing his response lines, this speech more closely resembles his later efforts rather than his earlier speeches. While there was a place or two where a longer pause or more emphasis on a question might have evoked a greater response, the overall use of timing in this speech cannot be seriously faulted.

To listen to Kennedy delivering this speech is to be caught by the beauty of its language, and the challenge of the speaker. One is not aware of the delivery, at least not consciously. The true mark of the well delivered speech is when the delivery adds meaning and color to what is being said, but the listener is not aware that the delivery is doing so.

John F. Kennedy was an intelligent, responsible, effective speaker who, January 20, 1961, gave a memorable speech which is still considered one of the best inaugural speeches ever given as well as one of the finest examples of the beauty a speaker can achieve with the English language. These are two very good reasons for studying this speech. There is a third. We should realize that this speech was created and delivered by a man who began his public career as a poor public speaker, who did not like the speaking experience, but who not only learned how to deliver a memorable speech, but even to enjoy doing so.

Nicholas M. Cripe, Ph.D., is a professor emeritus at Butler University, Indianapolis, Indiana.

CRITICAL QUESTIONS

1. How does Kennedy's use of metaphors contribute to the effectiveness of the speech? For example, discuss his use of, "the torch being passed to a new generation," or "Now the trumpet summons us again."

2. What does the balancing of clauses such as "never negotiate out of fear, but let us never fear to negotiate" convey to the listener? What is the effect of a succession of sentences all constructed with antithetical clauses?

3. One of the most noted passages claims that "we shall pay any price, bear any burden, meet any hardship, support any friend, oppose any foe to assure the survival and the success of liberty." Does this passage signify an attitude that led to the disastrous policy of waging war in Viet Nam?

4. Notice the great diversity in sentence length in this speech. What is the shortest sentence? What is the long-

est? How many paragraphs contain only a single sentence?

5. Kennedy addresses more than one audience in this speech. Identify as many as possible. Why does he choose this strategy?

ADDITIONAL READINGS

Sorenson, Theodore **Kennedy** (New York: Harper & Row, 1965).

Sorenson, Theodore **The Kennedy Legacy** (New York, Macmillan, 1969).

Salinger, Pierre **With Kennedy** (Garden City, New Jersey: Doubleday, 1966).

Schlesinger, Arthur, Jr. **A Thousand Days** (Boston: Houghton Mifflin, 1965).

Kennedy, John Fitzgerald **Kennedy: A Compilation of Statements and Speeches Made During His Service in the United States Senate and House of Representatives** (Washington D.C.: U.S. Government Printing Office, 1964).

Parmit, Jack **The Struggles of John F. Kennedy** (New York: The Dial Press, 1980).

Collier, Peter & Davis Horowitz, **Kennedys** (New York: Summit Books, 1984).

NOTES

1. Theodore C. Sorensen, **Kennedy,** (New York: Harper and Row, Publishers, 1965), p. 24.
2. **Time,** November 7, 1960, p. 27.
3. Robert N. Bostrom,"I Give You A Man' — Kennedy's Speech for Adlai Stevenson," **Speech Monographs,** June 1968, p. 129.
4. See Sorensen, pp. 122-126 for an interesting account of this period.
5. Sorensen, p. 178.
6. Arthur M. Schlesinger, Jr., **A Thousand Days,** (Boston: Houghton Mifflin Company, 1965), p. 110.
7. Ralph G. Martin, **A Hero For Our Time,** (New York: Macmillan Publishing Co., 1983), p. 164.
8. Pierre Salinger, **With Kennedy,** (New York: Doubleday & Co., Inc., 1966), p. 331.
9. White, p. 364.
10. **Time,** January 27, 1961, p. 7.
11. Linkugal, Allen, Johannesen, **Contemporary American Speeches,** 2nd. ed., (Belmont, California: Wadsworth Publishing Co., Inc., 1969), p. 278.
12. Salinger, p. 109.
13. Salinger, p. 66.
14. James L. Golden, "John F. Kennedy and the 'Ghosts,'" **Quarterly Journal of Speech,** December 1966, p. 353.
15. Sorensen, p. 241.
16. *Ibid.*
17. Golden, p. 354.
18. *Ibid.*

Martin Luther King, Jr.
I Have A Dream

"from every hill and molehill . . . from every mountainside, let freedom ring."

CRITIC: Lloyd E. Rohler

To fully understand the signifiance of Martin Luther King's historic address, we must recall the position of blacks in American society in 1963. There was no national law forbidding discrimination in public places and only a few states and localities had statutes even approaching equality. Black Americans faced the public humiliation of being refused service at any eating establishment from the most humble greasy spoon to the most expensive restaurant. Travel presented a special nightmare. With most hotels and motels closed to them, black Americans drove long distances with no guarantee of finding even minimal comforts along the way. Discrimination existed in all sections of the country. Even in the supposedly more tolerant Northern states, black Americans never knew when a restaurant owner, obeying his own or his customer's prejudices, might decide not to serve them. The situation in the Southern states was particularly demeaning. There, the aftermath of Reconstruction left a legacy of "Jim Crow" statutes that mandated segregation in all public facilities. Separate entrances and exits in public buildings and separate seating arrangements on buses and trains were accompanied by signs reading "whites only" and "colored." All these measures assaulted the spirit and reinforced the idea of second class citizenship. In Southern communities, public recreation areas such as ball parks, swimming pools, and tennis courts paid for with taxes collected in part from black citizens were forbidden to them. Discriminatory voting practices including excessively difficult literacy tests prevented most black Americans residing in Southern states from voting. Denied their rights, and denied the legal means to redress these wrongs, black Americans confronted a "shameful condition."

Many Americans joined with religious leaders, civil rights organizations and prominent black and white civic leaders in calling for an end to this demeaning system. The election of John F. Kennedy in 1960 brought hope to this coalition. Personally committed to equal rights for all Americans, Kennedy received crucial support from black voters particularly in Illinois in his narrow victory over Richard Nixon. Worried that a confrontation over civil rights legislation with the Southern Senators and Representatives who dominated the major committees in Congress would doom his legislative program, Kennedy temporized for two years. Finally forced by racial strife in the South to take action, Kennedy proposed legislation to outlaw discrimination in public accommodations in a nationally televised address on June 11, 1963. He told the nation:

We are confronted with a moral issue. It is as old as the Scriptures and is as clear as the American Constitution.

The heart of the question is whether all Americans are to be afforded equal rights and equal opportunities, whether we are going to treat our fellow Americans as we want to be treated.[1]

While the President may propose legislation, Congress enacts it into law. Although public opinion polls showed widespread support for the proposed legislation and a majority of both the House and the Senate favored it, passage was far from certain. A determined minority using Senate rules that permit unlimited debate had in the past and could again, "filibuster" or talk a civil rights bill to death. Southern Senators suddenly discovered a myriad of questions about the bill — questions requiring extended examination and discussion. Civil rights leaders unwilling to see this excellent opportunity to pass a civil rights bill blocked by legislative manuevers, decided on the counter strategy of staging a massive protest march to demonstrate the importance of the issue.

A massive march on Washington to demonstrate support for civil rights legislation does not happen overnight. All through the summer of 1963, the organizers coped with the many details involved in such a vast undertaking. Working through sympathetic organizations such as the National Council of Churches and the United Automobile Workers Union, the leaders of the march assembled a coalition of over one hundred groups that not only supported the goals of the demonstration but contributed the necessary money and manpower to make it work. A staff of organizers chartered trains, buses, and airplanes to bring people to Washington; arranged for food to feed them; established emergency medical facilities; provided for security; coordinated coverage by the mass media; and even installed a sound system so that the marchers could hear the speeches. Public response exceeded expectations. The organizers optimistically predicted a crowd of 100,000 people; over 200,000 actually came to Washington for the march.

The actual march was only a short walk down the mall from the Washington Monument to the steps of the Lincoln Memorial where entertainers and then speakers aroused the crowd. Peter, Paul, and Mary, Bob Dylan and Joan Baez sang folk songs; Mahalia Jackson sang hymns. A long list of speakers including Senator Hubert Humphrey, UAW leader Walter Reuther, NAACP President Roy Wilkins, Urban League President Whitney Young, and other notables addressed the crowd. Each was to speak for only five minutes, but all of the speakers went overtime as the crowd basked in the sunshine, waded in the reflecting pool, and drifted away. It was almost 3:30 p.m. when A. Phillip Randolph introduced Martin Luther King as the "moral leader of our nation" and the crowd came to life and gave King a rousing welcome.[2]

THE SPEAKER

It was no accident that Martin Luther King spoke in the position of honor at the March on Washington, for he had become to both black and white Americans the symbol of the movement for civil rights. Born on January 15, 1929, in Atlanta, Georgia, Martin Luther King, Jr. grew up in a comfortable middle class family. Religion and education were important influences in the life of a child with a Baptist minister for a father and a school teacher for a mother. A precocious child, Martin graduated from Morehouse College at the age of 19 determined to pursue a career as a minister. He entered Crozer Seminary in Chester, Pennsylvania, and in 1951 graduated at the head of his class, winning a fellowship for advanced study in theology. Graduate study in theology at Boston University profoundly changed his life by deepening his understanding of the thought of Mohandas Ghandi and introducing him to the person of Coretta Scott whom he married in 1953. In 1954 he accepted the call of the Dexter Avenue Baptist Church in Montgomery, Alabama, to be their minister and served in that post until 1960. Shortly after his arrival in Montgomery, he became involved in the organization of the boycott against segregated buses. Elected President of the Montgomery Improvement Association, he became the chief spokesman for the black community during the boycott. He now discovered that he had been called to minister to more than the spiritual concerns of a single congregation and took the lead in organizing the Southern Christian Leadership Conference. The SCLC promoted direct nonviolent action to desegregate public facilities throughout the South and to end discriminatory voting practices. Confrontations in Selma and Birmingham drew world wide attention to the racial situation in the South. King's life was threatened, his house was bombed, and he was often arrested and jailed. At the same time his eloquence and his commitment to nonviolence won him numerous honors including Time magazine's designation of Man of the Year in 1963 and the Nobel Peace Prize in 1964. The passage of the Civil Rights Act of 1964 and the Voting Rights Act of 1965 changed the nature of King's campaigns. He focused more on economic issues involving jobs and housing, leading demonstrations in the North as well as the South. The growing claims of the Viet Nam War on the nation's resources and the resulting squeeze on programs to help the poor led King to speak against it in a series of sermons delivered in 1967. His new direction created tension within the civil rights leadership and angered old supporters in the Johnson Administration including the President. In 1968, while planning for a Poor People's March on Washington he traveled to Memphis, Tennessee, to support striking garbage workers. There, on the Fourth of April, 1968, he was assassinated.[3]

THE SPEECH

No speaker could wish for a more impressive setting for a speech. King spoke from the steps of the Lincoln Memorial facing a crowd of over 200,000 Americans that stretched before him around the reflecting pool and back toward the Washington Monument. In the distance he could see the dome of the Capitol Building; to his right, the Jefferson Monument; to his left, the approach to Key Bridge leading to Arlington National Cemetery.

King begins the speech with a reference to the magnificent setting and thus introduces the first major theme, the promise of the American Dream. He invokes the memory of Lincoln, the Great Emancipator, to contrast the historical promise of freedom with the present-day reality. The images that he uses, "a great beacon of light" and "joyous daybreak," underscore the bright promise of the dawn with the bleak reality of segregation, poverty, and exclusion from the mainstream of life. This theme is developed through the extended metaphor of a "check" or "promissory note" given to all Americans by the sacred symbols of our nation, the Founding Fathers, in the sacred texts of our land, the Declaration of Independence and the Constitution. These documents enshrine the promise of the American Dream of "life, liberty, and the pursuit of happiness." This promissory note which was given to all Americans has not been redeemed for citizens of color and thus it is necessary to remind white Americans of their sacred obligation to make it good.

King and his supporters have gathered at this "hallowed spot" to remind Americans not only of their obligation but of the "fierce urgency of now." In repeating the word "now" in the following sentences, he reminds the audience of how long the promise has awaited fulfillment. Again he uses images of movement and progress to indicate that the country should go "from the dark and desolate valley of segregation to the sunlit paths of racial justice" to make "justice a reality for all God's children." This phrase introduces a second theme that will be amplified throughout the rest of the speech — the brotherhood of man under the fatherhood of God. He does not directly develop that theme in this part of the speech but continues to discuss the "urgency of the moment" and to warn that "whirlwinds of revolt will continue to shake the foundation of our nation until the bright day of justice emerges." King is using the familiar carrot and stick strategy employed by many protest groups. He offers the carrot of "rest and tranquility" if the "negro is granted his citizenship rights" but warns of renewed distrubance to "business as usual" if he is not. In keeping with his commitment to non-violence and peaceful protest, King warns his followers against violence and hatred of whites, but his praise of the "marvelous new militancy which has engulfed the Negro community" is an implicit warning that there are others, more militant than he, waiting to challenge his strategy and leadership if it is not successful. Again he appeals to unity, claiming that freedom is indivisible and reminding blacks and whites of their common destiny in a shared land.

The formal text of the speech released to the press before the March and representing King's prepared remarks ends with a catalog of grievances and a reassurance that the situation will change. The grievances are specific examples of the general propositions asserted early in the speech. For example, police brutality is used to show that the lack of respect given to blacks as individuals makes them feel like exiles in their own land. King uses repetition of the word "satisfied" and parallel structure to build a climactic conclusion using a quotation from one of his favorite Hebew Prophets, Amos. On the tape of the speech, the viewer can see King look up from the manuscript, accept the applause of the crowd, and seemingly inspired by the moment begin to extemporize using passages taken from previous speeches, commonplaces taken from the Declaration of Independence, passages from the Bible, patriotic songs, and old Negro spirituals. He weaves all this material into a mosaic of the

American Dream with themes of peace and brotherhood and justice joining together to produce a "beautiful symphony of brotherhood" and national unity.

In this extemporized section of his speech, King is amplifying or expanding on the meaning of the American Dream using the traditional techniques of division, comparison, antithesis, progression, and accumulation. He begins by defining the American Dream as "all men are created equal" and dividing this basic concept into two parts; brotherhood and justice. He uses antithesis to compare the present with the promise of the future. He foresees the progression of Mississippi, a state "sweltering with the heat of injustice," into "an oasis of freedom and justice." He welcomes the day when his four little children will be judged not "by the color of their skin but by the content of their character." He further prophesies that even in the racially troubled state of Alabama, "little black boys and black girls will be able to join hands with little white boys and white girls as sisters and brothers."

He compares this dream of political and social change in America with a Biblical passage that uses antithetical phrasing to prophesy even greater change. He intimates that this is a logical progression of our common faith in the following passage which repeats the word "faith" four times in a series of antithetical sentences that contrast "a mountain of despair" with a "stone of hope," "jangling discords" with a "beautiful symphony," and ends in a series of phrases repeating and emphasizing the word "together." The repetition of the phrase and the rhythm of the words make a stirring refrain:

With this faith we will be able to work together, to pray together, to struggle together, to go to jail together, to stand up for freedom together, knowing that we will be free one day.

Again, King turns to a commonplace — a memory that the entire audience shares as he repeats a stanza of "America." Now that he had divided the American Dream into its two components and expanded upon their meaning, he progresses to the last segment of his speech designed to promote absolute identification between the ideas and the audience. This last section is an excellent example of the use of "accumulation" — a heaping up of details as a means of expanding upon the meaning of the American Dream and achieving unity with all the diverse segments of the audience.

He repeats the closing line of the song, "Let Freedom Ring" and takes it as a refrain repeating it as he invokes the images of the American landscape from the East to the West; from the North to the South. The geographic unity of the land parallels the unity of the people in one vast brotherhood of humanity. In the climactic conclusion of his speech, he unites the themes of brotherhood and justice into a magnificent image of all Americans united in a free land. Utilizing emotional appeals, he brings his speech to a triumphant conclusion that proceeds from the idea of the American land — "every village and hamlet, every state and city," to the idea of brotherhood — "all of God's children, black, white, Jew, Gentile, Protestant, and Catholic" — to the idea of Freedom and the American Dream — "Free at last! Free at last! Thank God Almight, we are free at last!"[4]

King's physical action is restrained throughout the speech. He relies on vocal inflections, pauses, and facial expressions to convey emphasis. Occasionally he turns his head from side to side or nods to emphasize a word or phrase. The voice is rather high pitched, sounding at times almost melancholy. During the first part of the speech he uses a text, and obviously looks to the text, to the audience and back to the text again. Throughout this process, he maintains good eye contact with the audience. When he comes to the "I have a dream" section, he is no longer reading from a text but extemporizing his lines. His manner becomes more animated and his gaze is more completely focused on the audience. His gestures are still somewhat restrained. Not until he denounces Governor George Wallace does he raise his hand above the lecturn. From that movement on, he becomes totally involved in the speech. He casts his eyes to heaven when he recites the words to "America" as though looking up to God. When he calls for freedom to ring from the "curvaceous slopes of California" his eyes are looking skyward as if to see the very peaks themselves. As he gathers momentum for the final appeals for unity for all Americans, his face and body convey the energy and excitement of the ideas and his arms are raised in an inclusive gesture as though he is gathering all Americans into his grasp. When he reaches the climactic phase "all of God's children," he dramatically throws his right hand upward and sweeps in an arc those gathered before him and symbolically all Americans who are included in his prayer for unity.

An experienced preacher, King knew the importance of preparing the audience for an emotional conclusion. Twice earlier in the speech, he aroused the emotions of the audience without permitting them the full satisfaction of releasing their pent up feelings. Very early in the speech, he used the repetition of the phrase, "now is the time," to bring the audience to an emotional plateau; but he quickly shifted the mood to a somber discussion of the responsibilities of the protesters to avoid violence. After another passage using repetition and parallel structure to catalog the injustices suffered by black Americans, King aroused the audience by building to an emotional quotation from Amos, "we are not satisfied, and we will not be satisfied until justice rolls down like waters and righteousness like a mighty stream." In gradually engaging the emotions of the audience, King created the condition for a tremendous surge of feeling when he ended his speech with the climactic vision of all God's children joining together to celebrate the reality of the American Dream.

We see King frequently interrupted by applause. The tumultuous reaction of the crowd to his climactic plea to "Let freedom ring" stands today as one of the most electrifying rhetorical moments in recent history. When the leaders of the March met with President Kennedy afterward at the White House, the President greeted them warmly and, shaking hands with King, repeated the phrase, "I have a dream."[5]

The media reacted with universal praise. **Life** proclaimed King's speech, "the strongest of the day" and praised the March as "an astonishingly well executed product of leadership."[6] **Newsweek** said it was "the emotional crescendo of an emotional day."[7] **Time** proclaimed it as "triumph."[8] James Baldwin captured the overwhelming sentiment: "that day, for a moment, it almost seemed that we stood on a height and could see our inheritance."[9] Murray Kemptom saw clearly the role that memory played in the speech when he wrote that, "the Negro moves us most when he touches our memory."[10]

Since that day, the speech has gradually been recognized as a classic American document — a statement of the vision of America shared by all her people. It has been widely reprinted in textbooks, reproduced on records, and often excerpted in televised documentaries. The words have become familiar to most Americans and many can recite a line from the "I have a dream" sequence.

The March passed into memory as one of the shining moments of the civil rights movement when black and white Americans stood together united in a vision of justice and brotherhood. It is difficult to assess the impact of either the speech or the March on the passage of the civil rights legislation. Shortly after that August day, President John F. Kennedy traveled to Dallas, Texas, where an assassin's bullet made him a martyr. President Johnson urged passage of the Civil Rights Bill as a tribute to the slain leader and signed the legislation into law on July 2, 1964. In King's words, the March on Washington "subpoenaed the conscience of a nation" and strengthened public sentiment favoring equal rights for all Americans.

Lloyd E. Rohler, Ph.D., is an assistant professor at the University of North Carolina-Wilmington.

CRITICAL QUESTIONS

1. List the various audiences Dr. King was addressing. Which, do you feel, was his primary audience and why?

2. Dr. King employs various geographical references: North and South, urban and rural, even eleven different States by name. What purpose does this technique serve?

3. Some of his contemporaries in the civil rights movement criticized King for his naiveté, i.e. his belief that the white community would succumb to moral appeals. How does

he answer his critics? Has history supported King's arguments?

4. Having examined speeches by Kennedy and King, what similarities in style and arrangement are apparent in both speeches? How are they dissimilar?

ADDITIONAL READINGS

Bennett, Lerone, Jr. **What Manner of Man: A Biography of Martin Luther King, Jr.** (Chicago: Johnson Publishing Co., 1964; 1968).

Clark, Kenneth B. ed. **The Negro Protest** (Boston: Beacon, 1963).

Garrow, David J. **Protest at Selma, Martin Luther King, Jr. and the Voting Rights Act of 1965.** (New Haven: Yale University Press, 1978).

King, Martin Luther, Jr. **The Measure of a Man** (Philadelphia: United Church Press, 1958).

__ **Strength to Love** (New York: Harper and Row, 1963).

__ **Stride Toward Freedom: The Montgomery Story** (New York: Harper and Row, 1958).

__ **The Trumpet of Conscience** (New York: Harper and Row, 1968).

__ **Where Do We Go From Here: Chaos or Community?** (New York: Harper and Row, 1967).

__ **Why We Can't Wait** (New York: Harper and Row, 1964).

Lomax, Louis E. **To Kill A Blackman** (Los Angeles: Holloway House, 1968).

Oates, Stephan B. **Let the Trumpet Sound. The Life of Martin Luther King, Jr.** (New York: Harper and Row, 1982).

NOTES

1. John F. Kennedy, "Television Address To the People, June 11, 1963" in Allen Nevins, ed. **The Burden and the Glory,** (New York: Harper and Row, 1964), p. 182.
2. Accounts of the March are contained in **Life,** August 23, 1963 and September 6, 1963; **Newsweek**, September 9, 1963; **Time,** August 30, 1963.
3. Stephan B. Oates, **Let the Trumpet Sound. The Life of Martin Luther King, Jr.** (New York: Harper and Row, 1982).
4. The complete text of the King speech appears in the Appendix of this book.
5. Oates, *Ibid.* p. 262.
6. **Life,** September 6, 1963, p. 22.
7. **Newsweek,** September 9, 1963, p. 13.
8. **Time,** September 6, 1963, p. 13.
9. Oates, *Ibid,* p. 262.
10. **New Republic,** September 11, 1963, p. 20.

Douglas MacArthur Farewell Address

"And like the old soldier of that ballad, I now close my military career and just fade away . . ."

CRITIC: Richard Jensen

On the morning of April 11, 1951, Americans heard the stunning news that: "their controversial and sorely beset President, Harry S Truman, had dismissed the majestic and almost legendary hero, General Douglas MacArthur."[1] In announcing MacArthur's dismissal, Truman stated:

With deep regret I have concluded that General of the Army Douglas MacArthur is unable to give his wholehearted support to the policies of the United States Government and the United Nations in his official duties . . . Full and vigorous debate on matters of national policy is a vital element in the constitutional system of free democracy. It is fundamental, however, that military commanders must be governed by the policies and directives issued to them in the manner provided by our laws and Constitution. In time of crisis, this consideration is particularly compelling.[2]

MacArthur's dismissal created a national uproar, with most Americans taking the General's side in the dispute. A Gallup Poll a week later found that sixty-two precent of the public opposed Truman's decision. More than 125,000 telegrams in support of MacArthur flooded Washington D.C. Political commentator Richard H. Rovere observed that, "It is doubtful if there has ever been in this country so violent and spontaneous a discharge of political passion."[3] There were even calls for the President's impeachment.

Following MacArthur's departure from Tokyo where 200,000 people lined the streets, he was welcomed by 500,000 people in San Francisco. Leaving San Francisco, MacArthur, "made a triumphant trip across the country, reminiscent of a victorious Roman general, and accepted the invitation to speak before both Houses of Congress — an unheard of procedure in American history."[4] MacArthur delivered his speech to Congress in an atmosphere of tremendous emotion and controversy. Carefully analyzed at the time, the speech continues to be studied more than thirty years later. To gain insight into the MacArthur speech, this chapter will briefly review MacArthur's life, describe the events leading to the speech, analyze the speech, and evaluate its effectiveness.

THE SPEAKER

Born in Little Rock, Arkansas, on January 20, 1888, Douglas MacArthur, the son of General Arthur MacArthur, grew up on various army posts throughout the country. Choosing to follow in his father's footsteps, he graduated from West Point in 1903 at the head of his class. After graduation MacArthur rose rapidly through the ranks while serving in the Philippines and Japan. During World War I he rose to Brigadier General, the youngest commander of a division in the American Army. After the war he served as Superintendent of West Point (1919-1922), Commander in the Philippines (1922-1925), and Army Chief of Staff (1930-1935). He returned to the Philippines in 1935 to organize the islands against Japanese aggression. Retiring briefly from 1939 to 1941, he returned to duty to head the defense of the Philippines against Japanese invasion. Forced to evacuate the Philippines, MacArthur proclaimed, "I Shall Return!" He escaped to Australia where he assumed command of Allied forces which eventually defeated Japan.

At the end of the war in the Pacific, MacArthur accepted the Japanese surrender aboard the U.S.S. Missouri. Named Supreme Commander of the Allied forces in Japan, Mac-

Arthur, "ruled Japan with — it is generally agreed — firmness, moderation, and sagacity."[5] In June of 1950 he was named Commander of the United Nations forces in South Korea, a position he held until relieved by Truman.

MacArthur's life changed greatly after retirement. His name "gradually dropped out of the headlines, and he passed the last decade of his life in relative obscurity." He encouraged supporters in an attempt to capture the Republican Presidential nomination in 1952, but was thwarted by the popularity of General Dwight Eisenhower. To large numbers of Americans, however, MacArthur remained a symbol of American military strength and traditions.[6]. MacArthur died in New York on April 5, 1964.

THE SPEECH CONTEXT

The Truman-MacArthur dispute involved the proper strategy for fighting the Korean War but grew out of profound differences about American foreign policy following World War II. After the war, the European powers were either exhausted or defeated; in Asia, Japan's military leaders surrendered unconditionally to superior American power and China remained deeply divided by civil war. Only the United States and the Soviet Union had the will and the power to influence conditions on a world-wide scale. When the Soviets showed signs of moving into Western Europe, the United States took the lead in organizing a series of military and economic alliances to contain the Soviet Union within its existing sphere of influence. American strategists viewed the weakness of Europe as a temporary consequence of the war and looked forward to the time when a revived Europe would again play a major role in world trade and assume responsibility for its own defense. In the meantime, the United States adopted a policy to preserve the balance of power in both Europe and Asia. The communist victory in the Chinese Revolution posed a serious challenge for this policy. American military planners now faced the nightmare of a coordinated attack by communist powers in both Europe and Asia. When North Korea attacked South Korea, many military leaders believed that the North Koreans were being used by the Soviets as pawns in a world-wide chess game to lure American forces away from Europe in preparation for a major Soviet invasion. Given the uncertainties of the situation and the almost hysterical alarm generated by the domestic anti-communist crusade of Senator Joseph McCarthy, American policy planners faced difficult decisions. A massive response to the North Korean invasion might involve the United States in a war of attrition with the numerically superior forces of China; use of atomic weapons might encourage the Soviets to respond in kind; and weakening the defense of Europe might lead to Soviet pressure on our allies. In the end the United States had the good fortune to obtain the approval and the participation of the United Nations in its efforts to repel the North Korean invasion. Using a strategy combining diplomacy and propaganda, the United States isolated the North Koreans and later the Chinese while waging a limited war in Korea and strengthening its position in Europe.

Unfortunately this policy was not an easy one to explain in the superheated political climate of 1951. The Republicans, who had not won a national election since 1932, were desperate for victory. When Truman upset Dewey in 1948, many Republican leaders feared that their party might be condemed to minority status for the foreseeable future. Events now handed them a great opportunity to win the Presidency and possibly the control of Congress with an unpopular war rapidly becoming a political issue. In the midst of this political turmoil, General Douglas MacArthur, the commanding general in the field, began to criticize the conduct of the war and to disagree with the policy and the strategy of the civilians in the State and Defense Departments.

The first disagreement arose over MacArthur's desire to use Chinese Nationalist troops from Formosa to fight in Korea. The President refused because he felt this action might provoke China to enter on the North Korean side. He, therefore, sent Averell Harriman to Tokyo to explain the administration's policy to MacArthur. Harriman reported that while MacArthur understood the reasons for the administration's decisions, he nonetheless continued to harbor a "feeling of concern and uneasiness that the situation in the Far

East was little understood and mistakenly downgraded in high circles in Washington."[7]

On August 28, MacArthur again created difficulties with Washington by sending a message to the National Commander of the Veterans of Foreign Wars outlining his views on the war. The administration saw the message as a public challenge to its policy, and Truman considered relieving MacArthur.

In a final effort to restore harmony President Truman decided to have a personal talk with MacArthur at Wake Island on October 15, 1950. Truman left the meeting thinking that MacArthur understood and supported his position. MacArthur, to the contrary, believed even more strongly that in matters of the Far East Truman, "knew little, presenting a strange combination of distorted history and vague hopes that somehow, some way, we could do something to help those struggling against communism."[8]

In November of 1950 the Chinese entered the war on North Korean's side, forcing United Nation troops on the defensive. MacArthur again called for the use of troops from Taiwan and requested permission to bomb Chinese targets in Manchuria. Truman ordered MacArthur not to cross the Yalu River, the border between North Korea and China. Instead of accepting the President's orders, MacArthur publicly disagreed with administration policy.

Dismayed by MacArthur's actions, Truman ordered him to make no further public statements unless cleared by the administration. MacArthur continued to speak out in direct violation of Presidential orders. Eventually the disagreement became the focus of partisan politics. The Republican Minority Leader of the House of Representatives, Joseph W. Martin, delivered a speech on February 12, 1951, in which he defended MacArthur's position. During the next few months Republicans used the public disagreement between the general and the president to attack the administration's policy in Korea. On April 5, 1951, Martin again read letters from MacArthur on the floor of the House of Representatives. The letters severely citicized Truman's policies.[9] Those letters, along with other statements by MacArthur, led Truman to believe that MacArthur was guilty of insubordination and on

April 11, 1951, he fired the general. In defending his action Truman said:

> If there is one basic element in our Constitution, it is civilian control of the military. Policies are to be made by the elected officials, not by generals or admirals. Yet time and again General MacArthur has shown that he was unwilling to accept the policies of the administration. By his repeated public statements he was not only confusing our allies as to the true course of our policies but, in fact, was also setting his policies against the President's.[10]

THE OCCASION

On the day of the speech MacArthur was escorted into the House of Representatives Chamber by Congressman McCormack, Martin, Vinson, Halleck, and Brooks, and Senators McFarland, Connally, Russell, Wherry, Bridges, and Wiley. MacArthur was introduced by the Speaker of the House, Sam Rayburn. On the day of the speech the seventy-one year old MacArthur was "vigorous, erect, and dignified" with the bearing of a man accustomed by fifty-two years in the military to commanding obedience. Those who listened to the broadcast did not get an impression of arrogance, but of a man "gravely concerned and genuinely sincere in his apprehension for the nation that had granted him the highest military honors."[11]

The speech was heard not only by those in the House Chamber but by a radio and television audience estimated at 49 million, an enormous audience at that time. As the first major address to be delivered to a combined radio and television audience it had enormous impact: "Ball parks were empty. The Boston marathon, which usually attracts a quarter of a million spectators, had less than half that number, and most of them were equipped with radios. Work in stores, offices, and factories stopped as men and women everywhere listened."[12] The speech also received extensive coverage in newspapers and news magazines.

THE SPEECH

As he approached this well publicized occasion, MacArthur enjoyed the reputation of being one of America's outstanding military orators. Few modern soldiers enjoy such a reputation, as they are generally restricted by discipline and convention from public debate. It is rare when public opinion calls forth extended testimony from even highly placed officers while they are serving the military.[13] MacArthur, to the contrary, has been described as "an orator by temperament, by habit, and by long exercise."[14]

Although MacArthur read the speech from a prepared text, he avoided the pitfalls often associated with that form of delivery. He made few mistakes in reading and maintained physical contact with the audience. One critic described his performance: "So perfect was his reading skill that he never made a significant stumble; so well did he familiarize himself with his manuscript that he was always in absolute control of his delivery and maintained eye contact with his audience as much as half the time during an address."[15]

MacArthur's delivery may have been somewhat affected by the reading, however. He started somewhat haltingly, emphasizing each word with about the same amount of force. His voice rose in energy and force when he stated, "under no circumstances must Formosa fall under Communist control," and later in the speech when he delivered the line for which he received the greatest applause: "I have been severly criticized in lay circles, principally abroad, despite my understanding that from a military standpoint the above views have been fully shared in the past by practically every military leader concerned with the Korean campaign, including our own Joint Chiefs of Staff."

A distinguished critic described MacArthur's voice as one "that sometimes rasped, seldom rose from a low flat pitch, yet swelled with resonant confidence."[16] Another saw him as "heroic in his bearing, movements, and gestures. His voice was by turns self-confident, convincing, stern, scornful, righteous."[17]

MacArthur's detractors did not see his bearing or delivery

as heroic but described him as an actor and showman who was called upon "to play before both Houses of Congress the part of the old soldier who did his duty as God gave him to see that duty."[18] Another critic called MacArthur "a mighty warrior, a showman conscious of the part he is playing and the destiny he seeks to fashion for himself."[19] His critics saw this speech as one more act in a lifelong attempt to create for himself an image of mythic proportions.

The organization of the speech is quite straight-forward. The introduction of the speech uses five paragraphs of text to establish a strong speaker-audience relationship by referring to the historic place where the speech is being given, and asking for a fair hearing from the audience. The body of the speech uses fifty-six paragraphs of text to justify MacArthur's dissent from official policy. MacArthur's plan was:

> . . . to narrow the listener's focus of attention, moving from (1) a brief consideration of the general world situation, to (2) a survey of recent social and political changes in Asia, to (3) a statement concerning the "strategic potential" of the Pacific area, and finally (4) a discussion of the Korean War itself.[20]

Throughout his dispute with President Truman, MacArthur claimed the administration did not understand the importance of Asia in American foreign policy. In the body of his speech MacArthur assumes the role of teacher — the lesson being that Congress and the American public must be less concerned with Europe and more concerned with Asia.

In the three concluding paragraphs of the speech, MacArthur emotionally appeals to the public to accept his views by invoking the sympathetic image of the old soldier who just fades away.

MacArthur uses simple unadorned language in the speech although some words like epicenter, littoral (sea shore), and salient (conspicuous or pointing outward) do not appear in everyday speech. He uses metaphors sparingly, referring to the Pacific Ocean as a "vast moat" and similes such as China being "like a cobra" ready to strike. At times he used vivid words such as "predatory" forces in the Pacific and the Chinese "lust" for power.

MacArthur's sentence structure added ornamentation to

the speech. The two most common devices used were antithesis (the contrast of opposites in the same sentence) and parallel structure (repeating phrases or words of identical or similar structure). Of the two, antithesis was the most common. A good example would be, "What they seek now is friendly guidance, understanding, and support, not imperious direction; the dignity of equality, not the shame of subjugation." An example of parallel structure would be, "This created a new war and an entirely new situation — a situation not contemplated when our forces were committed against the North Korean invaders — a situation which called for new decisions in the diplomatic sphere to permit the realistic adjustment of military strategy."

MacArthur also added interest to his speech through the balancing of good and evil. The Soviet Union, China, and North Korea are evil; the United States, Taiwan, South Korea, and Japan evoke positive images.

Perhaps the most striking aspect of the speech was MacArthur's use of proof: "Rarely have the American people heard a speech so strong in the tone of personal authority."[21] Thus MacArthur based vitually his entire speech on his personal ethos. A. Craig Baird identified this strategy as central to the "vindication of his intellectual integrity, wisdom, and good will."[22] Viewed by many as one of the greatest military heroes in American history, MacArthur continually invoked that image. The speech contains constant references to "I", and the only quotation used in the entire speech is from a previous speech MacArthur made in 1945! At times he refers to agreement with his views by military experts, but he never names those experts or directly quotes them. Thus MacArthur asks the audience to accept his ideas solely on his personal reputation and accomplishments.

Critics argued that this heavy emphasis on ethos reduced the effectiveness of the speech: "There is an appeal to himself as authority which places an enormous burden on his admittedly strong ethos and seduces him from logical development of issues."[23] The logical development of the speech consists of the listing of major ideas with the expectation that the audience will accept them because of his ethos.

The speech also appealed to emotion as strongly as any

prominent speech in the post-war era.

> *Here was the old soldier in the fading twilight of life still seeking at the end of a career of fifty two years in the Army to serve his country . . . Here was the veteran warrior recalling his boyish hopes and dreams on the plain at West Point a half-century earlier, and concluding his speech in part from the words of a popular barracks ballad of his youth.*[24]

The appeal must have been effective, as one observer noted, "At many times during the speech there was hardly a dry eye in the entire audience — so emotional was its impact."[25]

EFFECT

> *Following the speech MacArthur rode down Pennsylvania Avenue to the Washington Monument under an air cover of jet fighters and bombers flying in formation. In ceremonies held on the Mall he was presented with . . . the official key to the city while a 17 gun salute boomed out.*[26]

One of the most difficult things for a critic to discover is the effect that a speech has after its delivery, particularly when studying a controversial figure like General Douglas MacArthur. During his lifetime there was "no more controversial character" in the United States.[27] To his followers he was "magnetic, handsome, charming, colorful, persuasive, a military genius and prophet, a statesman without peer . . . For those who believe in him, his ethical and pathetic appeals were unmatched by those of any living speaker."[28] On the other hand, those who were not his supporters believed, "the General to be an egomaniac with a 'God' complex, an authoritarian who strives for the sole spotlight and who tolerates no disagreement, his ethical appeal is entirely negative and his emotional appeals are considered to be merely acting. He has been described as a consummate 'ham.'"[29]

Those who supported MacArthur praised the speech. Representative Dewey Short proclaimed that, "We saw a great hunk of God in the flesh, and we heard the voice of God."[30] In a more moderate vein Representative Joseph W. Martin, Jr. stated that the speech "was a masterpiece of context and delivery, possibly the great address of our times." The speech not only "'sounded' in a masterly fashion, it 'reads' even better. Each sentence is freighted with thought, each word is at work. Its logic, its simple directness, its clear-cut statement of the issues, and its orderly exposition makes the structure of the speech a model to follow. It was a monumental effort."[31]

Opponents described the speech as being mediocre in composition with some expressions which "would not pass muster in a college freshman class."[32] Critics also attacked MacArthur's knowledge of history, his concern for building his own image, and lack of logic to prove that the speech was a failure. Philip Wylie summarized: "It was confidently predicted that what MacArthur said 'would take a place beside Washington's Farewell Address and Lincoln's short speech at Gettysburg' . . . Then MacArthur spoke — and a week later no one could accurately recall a paragraph."[33]

From these quotations it is apparent that a case can be made for the speech as either a great success or a failure. Each person who hears or reads the speech should carefully evaluate it in light of the period in which it was given and come to their own conclusions. At the very least, critics must admit that the speech did strike certain chords in Americans because it is still read, discussed, and quoted. His most memorable line, "old soldiers never die, they just fade away," has become a prominent part of American folklore.

Richard Jensen, Ph.D., is an associate professor at the University of New Mexico.

CRITICAL QUESTIONS

1. What does the extensive reliance on ethical proof reveal about the speaker's image of himself? What does it say about his conception of the role the audience should play in judging the speech?

2. What events fresh in the memory of his audience would

make his warning against appeasement especially effective?

3. What is the purpose of quoting the lines from the barrack ballad? What are these lines supposed to signify to the audience about MacArthur?
4. Obviously this speech had a polarizing effect on the audience: critics called it both "mediocre" and a "masterpiece." Are these extreme reactions supportive or destructive of MacArthur's goals for the occasion?
5. Most important leaders read their speeches to limit potentially destructive errors. Compare MacArthur's style of manuscript reading with that of John Kennedy's. How does each speaker's familiarity (or lack of familiarity) affect their style?

ADDITIONAL READINGS

Gunther, John. **The Riddle of MacArthur, Japan, Korea, and the Far East** (New York: Harper 1951).

Lowitt, Richard. **The Truman-MacArthur Controversy** (Chicago: Rand McNally and Company, 1967).

MacArthur, Douglas. **Reminiscences.** (New York: McGraw-Hill Book Company, 1964).

Manchester, William R. **American Caesar, Douglas MacArthur, 1880-1964** (Boston: Little, Brown, 1978).

Rovere, Richard H. and Arthur M. Schlesinger, Jr. **The General and the President** (New York: Farrar, Strauss, 1951).

Spanier, John W. **The Truman-MacArthur Controversy and the Korean War** (Cambridge: Harvard University Press, 1959).

Wittner, Lawrence S. **MacArthur** (Englewood Cliffs, New Jersey: Prentice-Hall, Inc. 1971).

MacArthur's speech sparked a debate in the **Quarterly Journal of Speech**.Because each article responded to previous ones, the articles listed below are in the chronological order in which they appeared.

Haberman, Frederick W. "General MacArthur's Speech A Symposium of Critical Comment." **Quarterly Journal of Speech,** 37 (October 1951), 321-331.

Wylie, Philip, "Medievalism and the MacArthur Legend." **Quarterly Journal of Speech,** 37 (December 1951), 473-478.

Beall, Paul R., "Viper-Crusher Turns Dragon Slayer." **Quarterly Journal of Speech**, 37 (December 1951), 473-478.

Beaven, Winton H. "Douglas MacArthur." **Quarterly Journal of Speech**, 38 (October 1952), 270-272.

Wallace, Karl R., "On the Criticism of the MacArthur Speech." **Quarterly Journal of Speech**,39 (February 1953), 69-74.

NOTES

1. Richard Lowitt, "Introduction," in **The Truman-MacArthur Controversy**, ed. Richard Lowitt (Chicago: Rand McNally and Co., 1967), p. 1.
2. Harry S Truman, "Truman Relieves MacArthur of His Commands," in **MacArthur**, ed. Lawrence S. Wittner (Englewood Cliffs, New Jersey: Prentice-Hall, Inc., 1971), pp. 102-103.
3. Quoted in Douglas Ehninger, "Address to Congress," in **The Speaker's Resource Book**, ed. Carroll C. Arnold, Douglas Ehninger, and John C. Gerber (Glenview, Illinois: Scott Foresman and Co., 1961), p. 277.
4. Houston Peterson, "General Douglas MacArthur Defends His Conduct of the War in Korea," in **Treasury of the World's Great Speeches**, ed. Houston Peterson (New York: Simon and Schuster, Inc., 1965), p. 817.
5. Bower Aly and Lucile F. Aly, "Douglas MacArthur," in **Speeches in English**, ed. Bower Aly and Lucile Aly (New York: Random House, 1968), p. 244.
6. Wittner, *Ibid.* p. 125.
7. General Douglas MacArthur, quoted in Lowitt, p. 9.
8. General Douglas MacArthur, quoted in Lowitt, p. 17.
9. Martin's role in the controversy is discussed in Lowitt, pp. 42-44.
10. Harry S Truman, quoted in Lowitt, p. 41.
11. Aly and Aly, *Ibid.,* P. 247.
12. Ehninger, *Ibid.,* p. 278.
13. A. Craig Baird, quoted in Frederick Haberman's "General MacArthur's Speech: A Symposium of Critical Comment," in **Great American Speeches, 1898-1963**, ed. John Graham (New York: Appleton-Century-Crofts, 1970), p. 242.
14. Baird, quoted in Haberman, p. 242.
15. Winton H. Beaven, "Douglas MacArthur," in Graham, p. 259.
16. W. Norwood Brigance, quoted in Haberman, p. 238.
17. Baird, quoted in Haberman, p. 243.
18. Quincy Howe, quoted in Haberman, p. 236.

19. William T. Evjue, quoted in Haberman, p. 236.
20. Ehninger, *Ibid.,* p. 279.
21. Herbert A. Wichelns, quoted in Haberman, p. 239.
22. Baird, quoted in Haberman, pp. 242-243.
23. Graham, *Ibid.,* p. 88.
24. Howell, quoted in Haberman, p. 240.
25. Alexander Wiley, quoted in Haberman, p. 233.
26. Ehninger, *Ibid.,* p. 278.
27. Beaven, *Ibid.,* p. 260.
28. Beaven, *Ibid.,* p. 260.
29. Beaven, *Ibid.,* p. 260.
30. Dewey Short, quoted in Haberman, p. 229.
31. Joseph W. Martin, Jr. quoted in Haberman, p. 230.
32. Evjue, quoted in Haberman, p. 236.
33. Philip Wylie, "Medievalism and the MacArthur Legend," in Graham, p. 245.

Adolph Hitler
1934 Nazi Party Rally

"Expel what has proved to be rotten and therefore not of our kind."

CRITICS: Lloyd E. Rohler & J. Justin Gustainis

Forty years after his death, Adolph Hitler continues to exert a perverse fascination for our culture as the evil figure of the twentieth century. The daring of his ambition and the monstrosity of his imagination created untold human suffering and profoundly changed the political map of Europe and ultimately the world. Though far removed from Quintilian's ideal of the orator as the good man speaking well, Hitler's forceful delivery of emotional speeches to audiences conditioned by spectacular displays of military and patriotic symbols played a major role in his rise to power.

This essay examines Hitler's speech on the closing night of the Sixth Party Congress at Nuremberg on September 14, 1934. The purpose of the essay is to demonstrate the usefulness of the classical system in evaluating the speech of a man who rejected the concept of rational argument that is the very basis of classical rhetoric. This essay will demonstrate that the application of the classical categories can reveal the reasons for the overwhelming emotional response by the audiences as well as the ultimate weakness in Hitler's method of persuasion.

THE SPEAKER

Adolph Hitler was born in the Austrian town of Braunau on April 20, 1889, the son of a customs officer of the Austro-Hungarian Empire who would prove to be a domineering father. A mediocre student, young Hitler left high school at the age of sixteen without a diploma. Inclined to become an artist, Hitler spent his late adolescence in dreamy idleness. Refused admission to the Academy of Fine Arts in Vienna at the age of 18, disappointed and alienated, Hitler drifted and absorbed the ideas that would dominate his life: anti-Semitism, nationalism, celebration of the will, and the cult of violence. When Germany went to war in 1914, Hitler in a burst of patriotism enlisted in the German army. Serving in the front lines during the next few years, he was twice wounded and five times decorated for bravery. Temporarily blinded by a mustard gas attack in October of 1918, Hitler recuperated in the hospital when the armistice was declared. He remained in the army for several years after the war serving as a political instructor. As part of his duties, he monitored political organizations. While attending a meeting of the German Workers Party, he spoke so forcefully that he was invited to join. His talents were recognized, and he soon took charge of recruiting new members. Thanks to his organizational skills and his inspired oratory, party membership grew rapidly and so did Hitler's influence. Within a year, he became the party leader.

By 1923, some 50,000 dues paying members of the party made Hitler a force in German politics. Impressed by Mussolini's successful "March on Rome," Hitler attempted to take advantage of unsettled conditions in Bavaria to lead a "March on Berlin." The "Beer Hall Putsch," as the activities of November 8 and 9, 1923, are called, resulted in the death of several party members and in Hitler and his deputies being arrested and tried for treason. Hitler used his oratorical skills to turn the trial into a propaganda forum for the party and win the minimum sentence possible for himself. While in prison, he wrote the first volume of **Mein Kampf**, his autobiography. Released after serving only nine months of a five year term, Hitler returned to Munich to rebuild the party. The next years were not very successful, as the post-war prosperity robbed the party of much of its appeal, but the good times were soon to end. The world wide effects of the Great Depression improved Nazi prospects. Between 1928 and 1930, the party gained enough votes to go from 12 seats in the Reichstag to 107 and become the second largest political party in Germany. This increased political power led to increased respectability and financial support. In Germany in 1930 no party had a parliamentary majority, and attempts to form one floundered on political polarization between the left and the right. In the absence of a parliamentary majority, the Weimar Constitution empowered the President to use emergency powers to appoint a Chancellor who could rule by decree. President von Hindenberg used this expedient to form a centrist government, but agitation by the Nazi Party led to the calling of new elections in 1932 to remedy the situation. The new elections resulted in a stunning victory for Hitler and the Nazi party as their representation in the Reichstag grew to 230 seats making them the largest party in parliament. Although still lacking a majority of the votes, a new government would have to include them; and Hitler refused to join any government that did not give him the post of Chancellor. He calculated (correctly) that as Chancellor he would have the opportunity to manipulate the President, Field Marshall von Hindenburg, into issuing a decree giving him emergency powers. Aided by conservative nationalist politicians who thought that they could manipulate him, Hitler assumed office on January 30, 1933, and immediately set to work to subvert the legal institutions of Germany and to gather all power into his hands. In the wake of the mysterious burning of the Reichstag Building on the night of February 27, 1933, which the Nazi propagandists blamed on the communists, Hitler persuaded von Hindenburg to sign an emergency decree suspending indefinitely all the basic rights guaranteed in the constitution. A month later Hitler forced through the Reichstag an "Enabling Act" which gave him the power to enact legislation without parliamentary approval and to deviate from the constitution whenever he deemed it necessary. These two actions ended constitutional government in Germany and formed the basis for Hitler's dictatorship. Hitler moved quickly to use the emergency powers to destroy any independent power base that might challenge him and to bring all institutions in German society under the control of the Nazi Party. In the summer of 1934, in a bid to gain support of the Army, Hitler brought the paramilitary units of the Party, the Storm Troopers of the SA, under tighter control in a bloody purge. The death of von Hindenburg in August, 1934, allowed Hitler, a foreign born, poorly educated, ex-corporal, to assume the title of Head of State and Commander-in-Chief of the Armed Forces of Germany. This is the man who addressed the Party faithful at Nuremberg on September 14, 1934, and received their adulation as "Führer."[1]

OCCASION

The use of spectacle to arouse the emotions of the audience was not unknown in Ancient Greece or Rome. When Pericles gave the funeral oration for Greek soldiers killed in battle, he stood on the sacred ground surrounded by trophies of war and armed soldiers. Mark Antony's funeral oration for Julius Caesar depended for effect on the bloody evidence of the Assassination. However, no ancient rhetorical theorist could imagine the spectacle that an industrialized country in the 20th Century would be able to arrange. Classical theorists placed great emphasis upon the speech as an instrument of persuasion; Hitler demonstrated the importance of staging and spectacle to arouse the emotions of the audience and to heighten the effect of the speech.

The party rallies held in Nuremberg in September of each year were a good example of the use of spectacle by the Nazis and of the careful attention to detail that went into their production. The purpose of the rallies was to demonstrate to both Germany and the World the power and unity of the new German Reich. Party organizations and sections such as Hitler Youth, the SA, the SS, and party cadres from local bosses to regional directors, all got an opportunity to meet together, hear party directives, and parade before Hitler. Almost 500,000 persons from all over Germany would be brought to Nuremberg during the eight days in September to be indoctrinated in the new policies of the party and then sent back to their communities to spread the new line to others.[2]

Nuremberg, an ancient medieval town with Gothic cathedrals and gable roofed old houses, served as the setting for these rallies and symbolically united the old Germany with the new. Hitler always stayed at the Deutscher Hof where he frequently appeared on the balcony overlooking the moat in front of the hotel to receive the adulation of the crowd. His every appearance was carefully orchestrated for full dramatic effect. When he appeared at the opening meeting of the Party Congress at Luitpold Hall on the outskirts of the city, the vast auditorium was a sea of Nazi banners. A band that had been playing marching songs suddenly stopped. The crowd quieted, the band struck up the Bandenweiler March, and Hitler, Goring, Goebbels, Hess, and Himmler strode down the center aisle while 30,000 people stood at attention, hands raised in the Nazi salute. Hitler mounted the floodlit stage and took his place surrounded by hundreds of party officials. Draped on the wall behind him was the sacred standard carried in the streets of Munich during the attempted "putsch." It was stained with the blood of martyrs, and before Hitler spoke, Hess read the name of each martyr. Members of the audience wept.[3]

Nuremberg provided an ideal setting for the vast open air pageants staged at night and so beloved by Hitler. One evening over 200,000 party faithful crowded into the open air stadium. Over 20,000 flags unfurled to the night breeze and were illuminated by long search lights that stabbed the night. After the chanting, singing, and playing of patriotic music, Hitler entered the stadium to a deafening roar. Standing in the back of the car, he acknowledged the salutes of the crowd. The pagentry of the occasion swept the crowd into an emotional crescendo that reached hysteria when Hitler began to speak. Later over 15,000 party faithful marched in a torchlight parade through the streets of Nuremberg while Hitler reviewed them.[4]

The theme of the 1934 Party Congress, "The Party Day of Unity," assumed great importance for both leadership and rank and file members of the Nazi party that year. Three months earlier, in June, Hitler ordered a bloody purge of the party in which thousands were arrested and shot without trial including many long time associates from the early days in Munich. Hitler worried that the brown shirted Storm Troopers or SA lead by Ernst Roehm posed a threat to his leadership. The SA leadership recalled the days when the Party was the National Socialist Party and resented Hitler's growing alliance with German industrialists. Hitler in turn realized that the boozing, brawling SA, whose members were mostly drawn from the lower classes, threatened the vital support of the Army whose leadership reflected the conservative values of the upper class. As Hamilton Burder wrote in his study of the Nuremberg rallies: "The leaders of the army . . . regarded the SA as an association of hoodlums and street brawlers. Although Hitler felt indebted to the SA for having stood by him in the years of crisis, he was dependent on the Army to keep him in power."[5]

Thus, toward the end of June, Hitler acted. At his order, Roehm and the rest of the SA leadership were arrested by the SS (the "elite guard" units, which comprised the military arm of the party) and executed without trial. A figurehead, Viktor Lutze, was installed in Roehm's place and instructed to keep the SA in line. The 1934 party rally was to be the first real test of how well he had succeeded.

THE SPEECH

The classical rhetorical system reflects a rational world view. The members of the audience are rational persons capable of making decisions among competing policies, ideas, or claims, through an analysis of the proofs or evidence offered. Although classical theory recognizes that emotion and personal influence often play a role in the decision making process, it emphasizes that the speaker must provide rational arguments to satisfy the critical mind of the listener. The classical system strives for a balanced effect - an effective speech should satisfy the demand of the audience for good reasons that are emotionally compelling and given by a believable speaker. Using this system to evaluate Hitler's speech, we can identify his major strategy. Hitler relied on emotional proof and personal force to the total exclusion of rational argument. He theorized that the masses possessed essentially "feminine" characteristics and had an "emotional longing" for domination by a "ruthless and fanatical" speaker.[6] Acting on this assumption, his speeches were not designed to persuade by rational argument but to move audiences by "divining the hidden passions, resentments, and longings in their minds."[7] A speech by Hitler conveyed "an extraordinary impression of force, the immediacy of passion, the intensity of hatred, fury and menace."[8] Often working himself into a rage, he "appeared to lose all control of himself . . . screamed at the top of his voice, spitting out a stream of abuse, (and) waving his arms wildly."[9] He told the audience what it wanted to hear: "the great universal obvious hopes: that Germany should once again become what it had been, that the economy should function, that the farmer . . . the townsman, the worker, the employer . . . should forget their differences and become one in . . . the love for Germany."[10] His speeches became melodramas of the fight between good and evil moving from the perilous state of the present to a glorious triumph over Germany's enemies. And always, He - Adolph Hitler - der Führer, was the embodiment of the will of the people, the representative of the State, and the sole defender of the nation. The speech on the tape given to the closing session of the Party Congress at Nuremberg, September 14, 1934, is a good example of this technique. Evil is represented by the past - the old generation that grew up with the poisonous party politics of the corrupt parliamentary system. Unfortunately, some of those doubters found their way into the Party where their prejudices underminded its unity. Their "alien spirit" confused the "brain and heart" of the German people. Through vigilant actions of the party, those people have been weeded out of its ranks. This is the basic script of a melodrama - evil appeared, but good struggled with it and triumphed thanks to the leadership of Adoph Hitler. This is all nonsense, of course. It is Hitler's justification for ordering a bloody purge that left many of his old comrades dead - men who had been with him from the beginning in Munich and who now seemed a threat to his new respectability as Chancellor, and an irritant to his smooth dealings with the real source of power, the German Army. The purpose of the speech is to demonstrate to the German people and to the world that the Nazi Party is united behind Hitler's leadership. The speech will also provide an indirect justification for the recent purge that will suffice for loyal party members. Hitler does this in a very traditional way. He secures the good will of the audience by complimenting them as the elite of the German nation. He refers to them as "the best racial component of the nation," and later he says that "only the best National Socialists become party members." What does it mean to be part of the elite? For Hitler, it means three things: to be strong, to be pure, and to be young. Hitler's notion of strength is made clear when he refers to "the spectacular forcefulness of this imposing review of the armies of the party" and later when he says that the party members "will form and firm the German people and carry on their shoulders the German state and the German Reich." Purity means that the party members hold to the right ideas, "truly ideological," and possess "the very best German blood" in contrast to the Jews whose "unclean blood" polluted Germany. Hitler explicitly says that the party is aimed at the young, "Where the older generation might still waver, the youth is sworn to us and given to us, body and soul."

According to Hitler's address, this elitism of the party is achieved in two ways: by a selective recruitment and by weeding out undesirable elements. Hitler brings up the selectivity issue in several parts of the speech. Early in the speech, he reminds them of the legendary "days when it was difficult to be a National Socialitst . . . when our party comprised just seven people." Shortly thereafter, he claims "we mobilize the most valuable elements of fight and sacrifice in the nation, and they are never a majority but always a minority." And, still later, he proclaims that " . . . only the best National Socialists become party members."

The issue of purging certain deviant elements from the party is mentioned only once, but it is a clear reference to the housecleaning by bullets which the SA underwent a few months earlier. Hitler points out that, in the earlier days, the party was spared this task as political oppression eliminated weaker elements from the party; but "Now we must practice selectiveness ourselves and expel what has proved to be rotten and therefore not of our kind."

Thus, Hitler's message is essentially one of congratulation. The party members are congratulated for being part of a strong, young, and pure elite, which owes its status to the fact that it is a minority that is periodically purged of undesirables.

The delivery of the first part of the speech is restrained, almost matter-of-fact. In his speeches Hitler liked to build slowly toward a crescendo of passion whipping himself and his audience into hysteria. His voice was harsh and conveyed an extraordinary impression of force. The sound of the voice alone communicated an intensity of hatred, fury, and menace regardless of what he said. Hitler had an extraordinary talent for self-dramatization and for role playing. He could easily switch from one mood to another and be absolutely convincing. His gestures reflected his changing mood. At the beginning of the speech they are restrained. When he builds to an important point, they become vigorous and even threatening. He slashes the air with his hand or pounds the podium with his fist.

Whenever Hitler refers to "us" (meaning the Party), he touches himself or hits himself on the chest. This occurs every time he uses words like "we" or "us." Also, when he uses the word "leadership" he again touches himself. The message is clear. Hitler is the party; Hitler is the leader. The party has no leadership, no existence without him. The assembled party members have no existence without him.

EVALUATION

As the tape clearly indicates, this speech was a rousing success with the immediate audience. Afterward, when Hitler's sycophant, Rudolph Hess, shouted out the phrases, "Hitler is the Party! The Party is Hitler!" and "Hitler is Germany! Germany is Hitler!" the crowd roared its approval. Hitler achieved his goals: he got the adulation of the crowd and he got the demonstration of Party unity.

The Nazi leaders were greatly impressed with their ability to organize party rallies that produced mass hysteria. So impressed were they that Hitler personally chose Leni Riefenstahl to produce a feature length film of the Sixth Party Congress for use in propaganda efforts abroad. Hitler assumed that other audiences particularly those outside of Germany would be equally enthusiastic about the Nazi message. In this he was wrong. The audiences were impressed by the spectacle but shocked at the scenes of otherwise sensible people losing themselves in an emotional frenzy of adulation for a despotic dictator. In this case a message effective for a friendly audience was evaluated differently by an audience that retained its rational faculties. The film had a boomerang effect. It helped to solidify opposition to Hitler and his methods in the democratic states of Europe and in the United States. When people saw the irrational forces unleashed by the maniacal figure of Hitler, it made them understand the threat the Nazis posed to the values of Western Civilization. As the classical system postulates, man is a reasoning being. In the short run, his emotions may make him act foolishly; but to be effective over time, a persuasive message must include good reasons that can be critically evaluated by the audience. Hitler gambled that the irrational fears and hatreds of the audience magnified by spectacular displays of powerful symbols would be sufficient to overcome the rationality of the human mind. He and his audience paid a terrible price for that gamble when Allied troops marched into Berlin in April, 1945.

J. Justin Gustainis, Ph.D., is an assistant professor of speech at the State University of New York College - Plattsburgh.

CRITICAL QUESTIONS

1. Hitler spent hours practicing his elaborate dramatic gestures. How well did they serve his purposes? Would a similar style be effective today? Explain.

2. Touching or pointing to himself when referring to the collective "we" or the concept of "leadership" is one of Hitler's commonly used gestures. Can you identify others?

3. Hitler uses phrases such as "the very best German blood," and "expel what has proved to be rotten," and "not of our kind." Why do you think he chose to remain somewhat vague as to whom he was referring rather than identifying certain groups by name?

4. While he almost exclusively relies on what the Ancient Greeks called pathos, can you locate any instances where Hitler uses logos? Ethos?

ADDITIONAL READINGS

Bosmajian, Haig A., "Nazi Meetings: The Sprechabend, the Versaamlung, the Kungebung, the Feierstunde," **Southern Speech Communication Journal**, 31 (Summer, 1966), pp. 324-337.

Bosmajian, Haig A., "The Persuasiveness of Nazi Marching and Der Kampf Um Die Strausse," **Today's Speech**, 16 (November, 1968), pp. 17-22.

Bosmajian, Haig A., "The Sources and Nature of Adolph Hitler's Techniques of Persuasion," **Central States Speech Journal**, 25 (Winter, 1974), pp. 240-248.

Casmir, Fred L., "The Hitler I Heard," **Quarterly Journal of Speech**, 49 (February, 1963), pp. 8-16.

Casmir, Fred L., "Hitler, and His Audience," **Central States Speech Journal**, 15 (May, 1964), pp. 133-136.

Casmir, Fred L., "An Analysis of Hitler's January 30, 1941 Speech," **Western Speech**, 30 (Winter, 1966), pp. 96-106.

Delia, Jesse G., "Rhetoric in the Nazi Mind: Hitler's Theory of Persuasion," **Southern Speech Communication Journal**, 37 (Winter, 1971), pp. 136-149.

Lambertson, F.W., "Hitler, the Orator," **Quarterly Journal of Speech**, 28 (April, 1942), pp. 123-131.

Stuart, Charlotte L., "Architecture in Nazi Germany: A Rhetorical Perspective," **Western Journal of Speech Communication**, 30 (Fall, 1973), pp. 253-263.

NOTES

1. Allan Bullock, Hitler: **A Study in Tyranny** (New York: Harper and Row, 1962).
2. Hamilton T. Burden, **The Nuremberg party Rallies**, 1923-1939 (New York: Praeger, 1967), Chapter 1.
3. William L. Shirer, **Berlin Diary: The Journal of a Foreign Correspondent 1934-1941** (New York: Alfred A. Knopf, Inc.., 1941), pp. 16-21, 23.
4. *Ibid.*
5. Burden.
6. Alolph Hitler, **Mein Kampf**, trans. Ralph Manheim (Boston: Houghton Mifflin Co., 1943), pp. 337-338.
7. Bullock, pp. 372 ff.
8. *Ibid*.
9. *Ibid*.
10. Ernst Nolte, **Three Faces of Fasicsm: Action Francaise, Italian Fascism, National Socialism** trans. Lelia Vennewitz (New York: Holt, Rinehart and Winstron, Inc., 1966), pp. 292-293.

Franklin Roosevelt
1942 State of the Union

"The militarists of Berlin and Tokyo started this war. But the massed, angered forces of Common Humanity will finish it!"

CRITICS: Kurt W. Ritter & Lloyd E. Rohler

Many critics rank Franklin Delano Roosevelt as one of the most effective speakers of the 20th Century. Elected to the Presidency four times, he dominated the political scene of his time, leading the United States through the crisis of the Great Depression and the danger of World War II. If it can be said of anyone that he was destined to become a leader, Roosevelt is that man.

THE SPEAKER

Born January 30, 1882, and reared on the ancestral estate at Hyde Park, Franklin Delano Roosevelt had the benefit of an upper class education complete with private tutors, an exclusive preparatory school, and trips to Europe. Roosevelt graduated from Harvard with an undistinguished record in 1904. He attended Columbia University Law School and while studying law married Eleanor Roosevelt, a distant cousin, in a ceremony attended by their uncle, Theodore Roosevelt, President of the United States. Politics seemed a natural calling for a man of FDR's talent and family background; and following admission to the bar in 1907, he became active in opposing the Tammany Hall faction in the New York Democratic Party. His actions won him election to the New York Senate in 1910. An early supporter of Woodrow Wilson for the Presidency, Roosevelt was rewarded with the post of Assistant Secretary of the Navy following the Democratic victory in 1912. Recognition for his administrative talents and speaking ability gained him the Vice Presidential nomination on a ticket with Ohio Governor James Cox in 1920. Although the ticket lost, the campaign marked Roosevelt as a rising star in the Democratic Party. Tragedy struck in the summer of 1921 when he was stricken with polio while vacationing with his family. Paralyzed from the waist down, Roosevelt determined on a course of strenuous exercise to overcome his handicap and resume his political career. From this dark period of frustration and despair came a new confidence and optimistic spirit. Roosevelt reclaimed his place in national politics with a rousing speech nominating New York Governor Al Smith for the Presidency in 1924 as "the Happy Warrior." He followed this with such extensive political campaigning for the Democratic Party that he easily won the nomination and the Governorship of New York in 1928. His success in dealing with the problems created by the Great Depression in New York made him the leading candidate for the Democratic Presidential nomination in 1932. He won the nomination and the office with the campaign calling for a "New Deal." For the next eight years Roosevelt presided over a major transformation of the American economy while in Europe and Asia growing international tensions presaged war. Following the Japanese attack of Pearl Harbor, Roosevelt devoted his energies to defeating the Axis Powers and establishing a permanent system of security under the United Nations. He died of a massive cerebral hemorrhage at his retreat in Warm Springs, Georgia, on April 12, 1945.[1]

THE OCCASION

The occasion for this speech is a traditional one. The Constitution mandates that the President "shall from time to time give to the Congress information of the State of the

Union." From Thomas Jefferson until Woodrow Wilson, Presidents sent written messages to Congress. Roosevelt followed Wilson's example of appearing in person to deliver a spoken address to a joint session of Congress. On this occasion greater attention than usual focused on Roosevelt's message. This was his first major address to the nation following a fireside chat broadcast two days after the Declaration of War.

It may require some imagination for the contemporary student to understand the importance of this speech or the exceptionally positive reception given it. To many it may seem long and repetitive. However, if we put ourselves in the place of the audience who heard the speech in person or on the radio on January 6, 1942, we can appreciate more fully its impact.

Americans viewed with mixed feelings the growth of German and Italian militarism. Many were clearly moved by the plight of Ethiopia and the stirring speech of its Emperor Haile Selassie before the League of Nations appealing for aid. Many saw the rise of Hitler as a threat to American security. Another equally important segment of the American public thought the problems of Europe were none of our business. Many Americans, disillusioned with the peace settlement following World War I, drew the conclusion that the United States had been deceived into supporting the British and French through propaganda and the efforts of arms merchants seeking to insure payment for their goods. Legislation reflecting this mood restricted American business dealings with nations at war in an effort to maintain our neutrality. As Hitler demanded and got more territory — marching into the Rhineland in violation of the peace treaty, absorbing Austria, and annexing parts of Czechoslovakia — a major debate developed between those favoring neutrality and those supporting American aid to the democracies of Britain and France. This division among the American people seriously hampered an effective foreign policy and produced bitterness and rancor. The Japanese attack on Pearl Harbor silenced the debate as Americans rallied to the defense of the country, but deep divisions still remained over war aims and strategy. Some Americans and certain military leaders believed that we should concentrate our efforts in the Pacific where American interests and forces were under immediate threat. Others favored a unified strategy coordinating our forces with the other nations fighting the Axis Powers. This would give priority in military planning to Europe to prevent the Nazis from invading Britain and from consolidating their hold on the continent. A serious challenge to the Japanese in the Pacific would have to wait. Other questions troubled Americans. How much would the war cost? How should it be paid for? How much production should be shifted to war material and how much left for domestic needs? How were the social problems created by massive dislocations in the economy to be handled? These and other questions needed answers that only the President could give, and Roosevelt had not made a major policy speech discussing war aims or strategy in any detail. Thus, Americans eagerly awaited the State of the Union Address anticipating that some of their questions would be answered by the President.[2]

THE SPEECH

Without explicitly acknowledging that some Americans believed the United States should fight primarily, or even exclusively, where they had been attacked in the Pacific; FDR used two important arguments for unlimited participation in the war. First, he identified the Japanese with the other Axis powers; and second, he stressed that the success of the United States' war effort depended upon the success of the other Allied powers, including Britain and Russia.

Facing an audience outraged at Japan's sneak-attack on Pearl Harbor, Roosevelt opened his speech with a carefully developed analysis of Japan's methods and motives in war. Their method, he noted, was "the method of Hitler himself." Reviewing half a century of Japanese intrusions in Asia, he noted that "similar policy of criminal conquest (in Africa and the Mediterranean world) was adopted by Italy." Calling attention to the "Berlin-Rome-Tokyo alliance," FDR argued that the real purpose of the attack on Pearl Harbor was to distract America from the European conflict and give Germany time to consolidate its conquests. From the vantage point of history, FDR's remarks seem obvious, but in the context of January,

1942, this speech helped channel Americans' wrath so that it applied to Germany and Italy as well as to Japan.

A closely related argument centered on the need for the United States to provide significant material and military support to the Allied powers. The British Isles were characterized as "an essential fortress in this great world struggle." FDR portrayed America's interests as identical to those of Russia and China. The field of American military action, he declared, must not be limited to the Pacific; U. S. forces must be deployed so "we can strike at the common enemy wherever the greatest damage can be done him." To those who wanted America to gather its forces on its own shores for a defensive war, FDR declared: "We cannot wage this war in a defensive spirit . . . We shall carry the attack against the enemy . . . We must keep him far from our shores, for we intend to bring this battle to him on his own home grounds."

To an extraordinary degree, Roosevelt relied on the power of his personal authority in asserting that America would succeed. Military success remained a hope. Even increased military production was more dream than reality. Reason could support his calls for sacrifice as the only course for survival. Only his own reputation as a man who had led America through the crisis of the depression supported his claim that the war would end with an Allied victory: "It will end just as soon as we make it end, by our combined determination to fight through and work through until the end — the end of militarism in Germany and Italy and Japan. Most certainly we shall not settle for less."

Roosevelt called upon Americans to take their fate into their own hands by imitating the enormous sacrifices already made by the British, the Russians, the Chinese, and the Dutch. In the face of a protracted war that might even reach American shores, FDR declared: "No matter what our enemies, in their desperation, may attempt to do to us — we will say, as the people of London have said, 'We can take it.' And what's more, we can give it back — and we will give it back — with compound interest."

Instead of presenting a long list of initiatives, as is typical of State-of-the-Union Addresses, Roosevelt organized the entire speech in the "problem-solving" pattern. He devoted the first portion to defining the nature of the problem that America faced and stressing its global implications. After analyzing the problems created by the war, FDR presented his proposals for converting the domestic economy into a war economy and for launching American forces into the worldwide struggle. The third portion of the address was devoted to the problems the nation would face as it tried to carry out FDR's plans — the dangers of complacency, defeatism, and division within ranks.

FDR designed the speech to confront the American audience with the harsh realities of the nation's global enemy, and then to present an uncompromising statement of the personal sacrifices that would be required on the home front as America became the munitions factory and the bread basket for the entire Allied force. This would mean reducing civilian consumption of goods through rationing and taxes and long working hours as factories operated twenty-four hours a day, seven days a week. In short it meant "the dislocation of the lives and occupations of millions of our own people." To this awesome prospect, FDR added: "Let no man say it cannot be done. It must be done — and we have undertaken to do it."

An essential aspect of speech organization is the marshalling of supporting material to develop the main points of the speech. As you watch Roosevelt's speech, notice how he uses statistics. Once he began to list production goals for airplanes, tanks, anti-aircraft guns, merchant ships, and other arms, he ran the risk of confusing his audience with a sea of numbers. Notice that his points were most clear when he presented statistics in pairs (45,000 tanks this year and 75,000 tanks next year; 20,000 anti-aircraft guns this year and 35,000 next year). When he tried to compare three or more statistics, the resulting jumble of numbers seems to obscure his point:

> ... *in this year, 1942, we shall produce 60,000 planes, 10,000 more than the goal we set a year and a half ago. This includes 45,000 combat planes, bombers, dive bombers, pursuit planes. The rate increase will be maintained and continued so that next year, 1943, we shall*

produce 125,000 planes, including 100,000 combat planes.

A little later these statistics serve a useful purpose. In contrast to such large and impressive figures, Roosevelt stressed the small number of men who had defended Wake Island against the Japanese: "There were only some 400 United States Marines who in the heroic and historic defense of Wake Island inflicted such great losses on the enemy. Some of those men were killed in action; others are now prisoners of war." By personifying the war as a small group of men with which the audience could easily identify, FDR could emotionally declare: "When the survivors of that great fight are liberated and restored to their homes, they will learn that a hundred and thirty million of their fellow citizens have been inspired to render their full share of service and sacrifice." In one passage, Roosevelt painted the vivid picture of a small embattled band of soldiers and capitalized on the power of sharply contrasting two statistics: 400 fighting Marines and 130 million aroused citizens.

No matter how well arguments are supported with evidence, or how sound the persuasive strategy, a speech must be well written and delivered to succeed. In these areas FDR excelled. First, he carefully selected language that served his strategy of re-directing Americans' wrath to include Germany and Italy, rather than merely Japan. Second, he consistently employed a structure of language and soothing style of delivery which gave the audience a sense of continuity and stability. Hence, he achieved linguistically what could not be done through argument alone — a sense of stability amid turmoil.

FDR and his speechwriters recognized the power of language to classify and combine diverse elements. Once he had named the nation's opponents — Germany, Italy and Japan — he reinforced his persuasive goal of depicting a global (rather than an Asian) war for America by unifying all three Axis powers into a simple and singular "enemy." If he spoke of one, he spoke of all ("the Japanese and the Fascists and the Nazis"), but most often he spoke merely of "the dictators" or "the enemy." During the first third of the speech he used the plural pronoun to refer to the Axis powers:

> *They know that victory for us means victory for freedom. They know that victory for us means victory for . . . democracy . . . They know that victory for us means victory for religion. And they could not tolerate that.*

By the last third of the speech, Japan, Germany, and Italy were unified into a singular pronoun:

> *We must not underrate the enemy. He is powerful and cunning . . . He will stop at nothing . . . He has trained his people . . . For many years, He has prepared for this conflict . . .*

As a natural consequence of unifying Japan, Italy, and Germany into a single "enemy," FDR used language which unified all Americans. For every "they" and "he" used to refer to the enemy, Roosevelt used a "we" to refer to Americans. At times, it was difficult to determine when "we" referred to all Americans, or all peoples of the Allied nations — an ambiguity that further served FDR's persuasive goals.

As his address progressed, the stylistic contrast between "them" and "us" was transformed into a contrast between all evil and all good:

> *"brutal cynicism" and "unholy contempt for the human race"*
>
> *versus*
>
> *"the doctrine that all men are equal in the sight of God";*
>
> *versus*
>
> *"a world of tyranny and cruelty and serfdom"*
>
> *versus*
>
> *"the champions of tolerance, and decency, and freedom, and faith."*

Closely associated with the stylistic device of contrast was FDR's use of parallel structure. Time and again during the speech Roosevelt repeated the same linguistic structure from one sentence to the next, and to each succeeding sentence. Often this parallelism included the repetition of a key phrase or a key clause. During the first moments of his address he established the pattern:

> *We now know their choice of the time . . . We now know their choice of the place . . . We now know their choice of the method . . .*

With unrelenting repetition FDR continued this pattern to the very end of his speech, when he moved to his conclusion through a series of declarations:

We are fighting on the same side with the British people . . .

We are fighting on the same side with the Russian people . . .

We are fighting on the same side as the brave people of China . . .

Yes, we are fighting on the same side as the indomitable Dutch . . .

We are fighting on the same side as all the other Governments in exile, whom Hitler and all his armies and all his Gestapo have not been able to conquer.

This constant use of parallel structure and repetition provided a sense of stability, even inevitability, in the speech. One phrase followed another by an almost irrepressible logic. At least for the moment, the speech created linguistically and emotionally the sense of certainty which the American audience so badly needed to feel.

Although paralyzed from the waist down, Roosevelt gave the appearance of a vigorous man. He radiated energy and physical vitality. Usually speakers use movements of the arm, the torso, and the hand to convey physical vitality to an audience. Roosevelt needed to support himself at the podium with one hand while using the other to turn the pages of his manuscript. Too great a movement of his torso or the other hand would cause him to lose his balance and fall. It is remarkable testimony to his spirit that under such difficult conditions he managed to convey such great enthusiasm and vitality to the audience that many did not notice his physical disability. Denied the opportunity to use hand and arm gestures, Roosevelt compensated with an expressive face and a magnificently modulated and inflected voice. Refer to any passage on the tape of his speech, and you will hear his voice rising and falling, pausing, and changing tone to convey the meaning and the emotions of the words to the audience. These techniques of emphasis were exactly right for the new mass medium of radio that became a dominant force when he ran for the Governorship of New York in 1928. During this campaign he discovered that the inability to stride back and forth across the platform waving his hands and arms was no handicap when seated before a microphone that detected meaning in slight variations in the voice and broadcast those meanings to a mass audience. Roosevelt's mastery of the medium of radio enabled him to become an effective communicator and leader. Robert T. Oliver, a distinguished Professor of Speech, called his voice, "the best modulated radio voice in public life."[3] Listening to him on the radio, Americans felt that they were in the presence of a friend who was speaking directly to them in a relaxed and friendly manner. He spoke slowly — usually at about 100-150 words per minute — and employed frequent pauses.[4] He was superb at reading the lines of his speeches to emphasize their rhetorical effects. He liked to employ parallel structure in his sentences and phrases and utilized repetition of patterns of intonation and inflection to emphasize the underlying structure for his listeners. He rarely stumbled over a line but when unexpectedly interrupted by audience reaction he was always ready with an ad lib or a quip. He had a quick wit and used it with devastating effect in his campaigns, often demoralizing his opposition with a deft line followed by the famous Roosevelt smile.

EVALUATION

The speech was well received by the contemporary audience. Time practically gushed over it: "In Britain there was a wave of elation. In the Axis countries there was a stunned silence — and then an uneasy denial that the program . . . could be carried out. In the United States that same program brought good tidings of hope."[5] The New Republic under the heading "FDR Gives Marching Orders," proclaimed that "President Roosevelt's annual message to Congress on the State of the Nation will rank as one of the great utterances of a leader whose State papers are already the most impressive in the history of the Presidency." The editorial writer complimented FDR for articulating "not only the power politics and military strategy of total war, but also the vast gulf that today separates the two causes." As an example of the moral gulf between the allies and the enemy, the writer cited FDR's "capacity to speak of the enemy in terms of intensity . . . without indulging in the hysterical violence and hate mongering of Hitler's speeches." He concludes, "these are brave words, bold words, heartening words."[6]

Roosevelt's speech successfully combined the three forms of proof into an effective structure to create support for his strategy for defeating the enemy and to persuade Americans to make the sacrifices needed for a long and difficult struggle. If today we do not share New Republic's estimate that this "utterance" ranks among his best, it is precisely because the policy was so successful in destroying the enemy that we have forgotten the fear and confusion of those perilous days.

It is instructive to compare the careers of the last two speakers on the tape, Hitler and Roosevelt. Each achieved power in the same year and each died in the same month that the war in Europe ended. As leaders, each faced the problems created by worldwide depression and war. One was the leader of a great democratic nation who used the means of mass communication at his disposal in an ethical and responsible way to persuade the audience to support his programs. The other played upon the fears and hatreds of his audience through hysterical emotional appeals reinforced by spectacle and terror. The results of their leadership were clearly visible to the entire world in April, 1945.

Kurt W. Ritter is an associate professor of speech at Texas A. & M. University.

CRITICAL QUESTIONS

1. Why does Roosevelt begin his speech by reminding his listeners of his warning made a year earlier: "When the dictators are ready to make war upon us, they will not wait for an act on our part."?

2. Why does Roosevelt claim optimistically, "It (the war) will end just as soon as we make it end," and then pessimistically, "We must face the fact of a hard war, a long war, a bloody war,

a costly war"? What dual purposes is he addressing?

3. Roosevelt employs many religious symbols and references. List a few of these. Why does he employ them so frequently in this particular speech?

4. Compare Roosevelt's use of ethos to MacArthur's. How are they similar and how do they differ?

ADDITIONAL READINGS

SPEECHES BY FRANKLIN D. ROOSEVELT:
"Fireside Chats": Texts of two of FDR's radio broadcasts are included in **Contemporary Forum: American Speeches on Twentieth Century Issues**, eds. Ernest J. Wrage and Barnet Baskerville (New York: Harper, 1962).
"Inaugural Addresses," 1933, 1937, 1941, and 1945: These speeches are conveniently collected in **Inaugural Addresses of the Presidents of the United States** (Washington, D.C.: GPO, 1974).

STUDIES OF FRANKLIN D. ROOSEVELT AS A SPEAKER:
Benson, Thomas W. "Inaugural Peace: Franklin D. Roosevelt's Last Speech," **Communication Monographs**, 36 (1969), 138-147.

Braden, Waldo W. "Roosevelt's Fireside Chats," **Communication Monographs**, 27 (1955) 290-302.

Brandenburg, Ernest and Waldo W. Braden, "Franklin D. Roosevelt," **History and Criticism of American Public Address**, Vol. III, ed. Marie Hochmuth (Nichols) (New York: Russell and Russell, 1955), 458-550.

Crowell, Laura, L. Leroy Cowperthwaite, and Ernest Brandenburg, "Franklin D. Roosevelt, A Study in Leadership Through Persuasion," **American Public Address**, ed. Loren Reid (Columbia: University of Missouri Press, 1961), 211-243.

Ryan, Halford Ross, "Roosevelt's First Inaugural: A Study of Technique," **American Rhetoric from Roosevelt to Reagan,** ed. Halford Ross Ryan (Prospect Heights, Illinois: Waveland Press, 1983), 6-22.

Zelko, Harold P., "Franklin D. Roosevelt's Rhythm in Rhetorical Style," **Quarterly Journal of Speech**, 28 (1942), 138-141.

NOTES

1. There are many good biographies of Roosevelt and studies of his policies. James MacGregor Burns, **Roosevelt: The Lion and the Fox** (New York: Harcourt, Brace, 1956) is useful for a study of Roosevelt's leadership.

2. Denis W. Brogan, **The Era of Franklin D. Roosevelt: A Chronical of the New Deal and Global War** (New Haven: Yale University Press, 1950).

3. Robert T. Oliver, "The Speech that Established Roosevelt's Reputation," **Quarterly Journal of Speech**, 31 (October 1945), p. 274.

4. Ernest S. Brandenburg and Waldo W. Braden, "Franklin D. Roosevelt's Voice and Pronunciation," **Quarterly Journal of Speech**, 38 (February 1952), p. 23-30.

5. **Time**, January 19, 1942.

6. **New Republic**, January 19, 1942, p. 70.

A Closing Word to the Student

The rhetorical schools in Ancient Greece and Rome taught students through the practice of imitation. Students imitated the teacher, learning from him the skills necessary to become an accomplished speaker. With the aid of the teacher, students studied model speeches, analyzing them to discover the principles of speech composition. Often the student would imitate a model speech by paraphrasing the main ideas into his own words or actually memorizing whole passages. Through close study of model speeches, the student gained a thorough understanding of style. Memorization furnished him a storehouse of words, phrases, and figures of speech that he could call upon to improve his own writing. Although this method of teaching public speaking is no longer practiced, the authors of these essays recommend to you a contemporary approach to imitation. By using the video tape and this book, the student can improve his own understanding of the process of speech composition and delivery. We do not advocate the slavish imitation of the style or delivery of these speakers, but we do believe that analysis and imitation of the oral style of these speeches will aid the student in developing his own sense of the rhythms of American English. Memorization of a few of the memorable lines from the speeches will give you, the student, a valuable resource to draw upon when composing your own speeches or on the occasion when you must make an impromptu speech.

The tape and this book contain much that is of value for the beginning speaker. The entire first chapter, outlining the classical system, provides a systematic approach to composing and delivering a speech. The essays help you isolate those techniques which have proven appeal. This closing chapter emphasizes and summarizes certain concepts that are most useful for the beginning speaker.

First, classical rhetoricians stressed the importance of invention — of discovering the proofs that constitute the substance of the speech. This is particularly important for beginning speakers whose attention is often exclusively focused on technique, and who must be reminded that delivery is a means to an end and not an end in itself. The five speakers on the tape display great variety in delivery skills. They are remembered today not for their technical skills in delivering a speech but for what they said. Obviously you are not in the responsible position of leading a great nation nor are you often called upon to address vast multitudes assembled on an important occasion. This does not mean that students should not take great care in preparing their speeches. Lacking the ethos of a national figure, students will have to work that much harder to achieve success.

Secondly, the tape reveals that there is no one magic formula for delivery — no single rule to guide a speaker in every situation. The tape does not suggest that every speaker should utilize his natural talents to maximize the effectiveness of his delivery. If a speaker is lacking in certain physical characteristics, he should utilize others to compensate for it. For example, Roosevelt, crippled from the waist down, had to hold onto the podium for support and could use only limited gestures. He compensated for his handicap with a magnificent voice that conveyed more vitality than most able-bodied speakers can. John Kennedy, a poor speaker when he began his campaign for the Presidency, improved through practice. Kennedy's delivery techniques differed greatly from Roosevelt's and King's — yet all three men moved audiences through the spoken word. Each speaker developed a technique that emphasized his strengths as a speaker while minimizing his weaknesses. This is the goal that all speakers should strive for and one that is attainable by student speakers as well as important public figures.

The tape does contain an important lesson about delivery for beginning speakers who often rush through the speech as quickly as possible. All the speakers on the tape use frequent pauses to emphasize key words or phrases. Roosevelt is a particularly good model for developing an effective oral style. He spoke slowly — taking time to pause to emphasize the underlying structure of his sentences or to give weight to a word or phrase. The importance of good vocal inflection and intonation is clearly demonstrated by his speech. As an exercise, students might imitate Roosevelt's vocal patterns with the aid of a tape recorder to permit monitoring of their own phrasing.

It should also be noted that delivery is greatly affected by the medium of communication being employed. Observe Roosevelt who was the first American leader to really understand the radio as a powerfully persuasive medium. The radio highlighted the voice itself and Roosevelt developed vocal techniques appropriate to the sensitive microphone. King and, to an extreme degree, Hitler spoke adeptly to large crowds. Utilizing sweeping gestures and an oratorical style of delivery, they projected imposing images to audience members even in the most remote section of the crowd. If Roosevelt "discovered" radio, Kennedy demonstrated that television would, for the foreseeable future, change the style of personal leadership. Cameras focusing closely on the speaker's face magnified, as never before possible, subtle but meaningful changes in expression. Even the speaker's eyes became a persuasive instrument. Those "windows to the soul" communicated as powerfully for Kennedy as the most sweeping gesture had for Hitler. Successful speakers adapt to the media. As you watch the tape, notice Hitler's frequent smug expressions. He ignored the camera, and its audience, playing only to his immediate gathering. He appears unable to adapt his style to accommodate both. Kennedy and King, on the other hand, appropriately address both the immediate and the television audience. Perhaps we should simply note that the task facing the modern speaker has been complicated by technological developments in communication. Hitler spent hours practicing gestures and projecting his voice. Today's speaker is well advised to employ gestures, but also to attend to such formerly less significant manifestations as eye movement. Some contend, for instance, that Nixon may have lost the close election to Kennedy because television, during the debates, portrayed him as "shifty-eyed."

The tape reveals the importance of developing a characteristic style or signature as a speaker. This does not mean that all of your speeches should sound the same. Different occasions call for different levels of formality. Nonetheless, style brands the speech with the speaker's own uniqueness. Each of the speakers on the tape developed a characteristic style that revealed much about him — his sense of who he was and what he wished to accomplish. Kennedy's grand style fitted his vision of the role that the United States should assume in the 1960's. He longed for the greatness that comes from daring to do great deeds. His challenges to Americans rang true to his sense of the kind of leader he wanted to be. King's evangelical style with its Biblical rhythms and quotations from old gospel songs and scripture reflected his background and his concern with moral values. Contrast his style with Hitler's forceful and violent tirades and you see more than a difference between two approaches to giving a speech. You see a difference in philosophies of life. Roosevelt's direct style is simplicity itself. Listening to Roosevelt, we hear a friend whose colloquial expressions and simple analogies inspire confidence. MacArthur sounds like a General. He is authoritative. He commands our consideration of his arguments which he marches one by one across the page of his manuscript and into our minds. Each of the speakers is different; each has a characteristic style. The style reveals the man behind the words and gives the words of the text the meaning of lived experience. Read each of the speeches; then watch the speaker deliver them. When read, Hitler's speech lacks the menace we feel while watching him. King's words read well indeed, but when he speaks of black and white children playing together we feel warmed by the "experience." Again, beginning speakers will lack the experience of these men; but each of us possesses a unique personality. Through the stylistic choices we make, we reveal personality and humanity to our audience. This does not mean that a speaker should search for a novel or outlandish personality to intrigue the audience. It is a plea for beginning speakers to be more aware of who they are and what they can bring to the speech situation that will make their message distinctive.

The importance of memory to a speaker is clearly revealed

on the tape of the King speech. Memory provides the speaker with important material he needs to construct a speech. Obviously, in this scientific age, a speaker must rely upon research to provide the solid grounding in fact that is the basis for any speech; but facts do not speak for themselves. They need a human voice to give them meaning by providing a context for interpreting them. The memory of the past — the accumulated wisdom of previous generations as revealed through myths, legends, proverbs, folklore, poetry, fables, sacred scriptures, and literature — grounds the speaker's ideas in the conventional wisdom of the audience. This is the basis for the frequent recommendation that beginning speakers buy a collection of quotations. Memorable lines help to unlock the past and demonstrate the continuity of human experience. Memory is improved by reading and writing: reading the best literature and writing down important ideas and expressions. This book and the tape are designed to aid the memory of the beginning speaker by giving him some ideas and expressions that will be useful in his own speeches. All beginning speakers must understand the importance of practice. One does not become a good speaker overnight. Constant effort is required. The speakers on the tape became effective through years of practice. Rhetorical scholars have documented the hard work that these men undertook to improve their public speaking skills. Public speaking is a skill that can be taught. Scholars and teachers have accumulated and organized in a systematic way a vast body of knowledge. This book presents some of that knowledge to you in an effort to stimulate your interest in the theory and practice of human communication. This book is designed as a starting point in your effort to learn more about how you can be a more effective public speaker.

Whether or not you ever find yourself practicing your skills regularly as a public speaker, we hope your in-depth study of these five speeches will make you a more critical consumer of persuasive appeals. An understanding of the tools of persuasion, identified by the Ancient Greeks as logos, pathos and ethos, may alert you to the legitimacy of a speaker's arguments and perhaps even his motives. The ability to look past Hitler's style and impartially consider how he supported his arguments might have saved millions of Germans the eventual destruction of their lives and homes, not to mention the devastation brought to those who suffered world-wide from his misadventures. Obviously, this is an extreme example, and you might even convince yourself you could never fall prey to such techniques. Nonetheless, the various media bombard us daily with persuasive appeals. Granted few are as malevolent as Hitler's were, but everyday we are asked to make critical decisions which affect how we spend our money and how we live our lives. We are asked to purchase a new car (it will enhance our image), attend a particular school or class (our career will profit), visit a certain locality on vacation (the people there are friendly and will attend to our needs), and to vote for a particular candidate (she can be trusted). While it may be true that we live in an age of communications, we must also realize that this age calls for decisions based on those communications, many of which are persuasive in nature.

Be a critic. Why is the speaker asking me to act in a certain manner? How well has he supported his arguments? What appeals did he rely on to gain my acceptance? Were those appeals relevant? Who is the speaker really addressing? We do not pretend to offer a simple method for answering these and other questions we have addressed in this book. Nor do we imply that we have provided all the right questions. The overriding skill we hope you will develop — as a speaker or a member of the audience — is the analytical approach of the critic. Be a critic of your own speech before you deliver it. Be a critic of those speeches you hear. Your performance will improve; the quality of your decision-making will improve.

APPENDIX:

COMPLETE TEXTS OF FIVE GREAT SPEECHES

INAUGURAL ADDRESS
John F. Kennedy

Vice President Johnson, Mr. Speaker, Mr. Chief Justice, President Eisenhower, Vice President Nixon, Reverend Clergy, Fellow Citizens:

We observe today not a victory of party but a celebration of freedom — symbolizing an end as well as a beginning — signifying renewal as well as change. For I have sworn before you and Almighty God the same solemn oath our forebears prescribed nearly a century and three quarters ago.

The world is very different now. For man holds in his mortal hands the power to abolish all forms of human poverty and all forms of human life. And yet the same revolutionary beliefs for which our forebears fought are still at issue around the globe — the belief that the rights of man come not from the generosity of the state but from the hand of God.

We dare not forget today that we are the heirs of that first revolution. Let the word go forth from this time and place, to friend and foe alike, that the torch has been passed to a new generation of Americans — born in this century, tempered by war, disciplined by a hard and bitter peace, proud of our ancient heritage — and unwilling to witness or permit the slow undoing of those human rights to which this nation has always been committed, and to which we are committed today, at home and around the world.

Let every nation know, whether it wishes us well or ill, that we shall pay any price, bear any burden, meet any hardship, support any friend or oppose any foe to assure the survival and the success of liberty.

This much we pledge — and more.

To those old allies whose cultural and spiritual origins we share, we pledge the loyalty of faithful friends. United, there is little we cannot do in a host of cooperative ventures. Divided, there is little we can do — for we dare not meet a powerful challenge at odds and split asunder.

To those new states whom we welcome to the ranks of the free, we pledge our word that one form of colonial control shall not have passed away merely to be replaced by a far more iron tyranny. We shall not always expect to find them supporting our view.

But we shall always hope to find them strongly supporting their own freedom — and to remember that, in the past, those who foolishly sought power by riding the back of the tiger ended up inside.

To those people in the huts and villages of half the globe struggling to break the bonds of mass misery, we pledge our best efforts to help them help themselves, for whatever period is required — not because the Communists may be doing it, not because we seek their votes, but because it is right. If a free society cannot help the many who are poor, it cannot save the few who are rich.

To our sister republics south of our border, we offer a special pledge — to convert our good words into good deeds — in a new alliance for progress — to assist free men and free governments in casting off the chains of poverty. But this peaceful revolution of hope cannot become the prey of hostile powers. Let all our neighbors know that we shall join with them to oppose aggression or subversion anywhere in the Americas. And let every other power know that this hemisphere intends to remain the master of its own house.

To that world assembly of sovereign states, the United Nations, our last best hope in an age where the instruments of war have far outpaced the instruments of peace, we renew our pledge of support — to prevent it from becoming merely a forum for invective — to strengthen its shield of the new and the weak — and to enlarge the area in which its writ may run.

Finally, to those nations who would make themselves our adversary, we offer not a pledge but a request: That both sides begin anew the quest for peace, before the dark powers of destruction unleashed by science engulf all humanity in planned or accidental self-destruction.

We dare not tempt them with weakness. For only when our arms are sufficient beyond doubt can we be certain beyond doubt that they will never be employed.

But neither can two great and powerful groups of nations take comfort from our present course — both sides overburdened by the cost of modern weapons, both rightly alarmed by the steady spread of the deadly atom, yet both racing to alter that uncertain balance of terror that stays the hand of mankind's final war.

So let us begin anew — remembering on both sides that civility is not a sign of weakness, and sincerity is always subject to proof. Let us never negotiate out of fear. But let us never fear to negotiate.

Let both sides explore what problems unite us instead of belaboring those problems which divide us.

Let both sides, for the first time, formulate serious and precise proposals for the inspection and control of arms — and bring the absolute power to destroy other nations under the absolute control of all nations.

Let both sides seek to invoke the wonders of science instead of its terrors. Together let us explore the stars, conquer the deserts, eradicate disease, tap the ocean depths and encourage the arts and commerce.

Let both sides unite to heed in all corners of the earth the command of Isaiah — to "undo the heavy burdens . . . (and) let the oppressed go free."

And if a beachhead of cooperation may push back the jungle of suspicion, let both sides join in creating a new endeavor: not a new balance of power, but a new world of law, where the strong are just and the weak secure and the peace preserved.

All this will not be finished in the first one hundred days. Nor will it be finished in the first one thousand days, nor in the life of this administration, nor even perhaps in our lifetime on this planet. But let us begin.

In your hands, my fellow citizens, more than mine, will rest the final success or failure of our course. Since this country was founded, each generation of Americans has been summoned to give testimony to its national loyalty. The graves of young Americans who answered the call to service surround the globe.

Now the trumpet summons us again — not as a call to bear arms, though arms we need — not as a call to battle, though embattled we are — but a call to bear the burden of a long twilight struggle, year in and year out, "rejoicing in hope, patient in tribulation" — a struggle against the common enemies of man: Tyranny, poverty, disease and war itself.

Can we forge against these enemies a grand and global alliance, North and South, East and West, that can assure a more fruitful life for all mankind? Will you join in that historic effort?

In the long history of the world, only a few generations have been granted the role of defending freedom in its hour of maximum danger.

I do not shrink from this responsibility — I welcome it. I do not believe that any of us would exchange places with any other people or any other generation. The energy, the faith, the devotion which we bring to this endeavor will light our country and all who serve it — and the glow from that fire can truly light the world.

And so, my fellow Americans: ask not what your country can do for you — ask what you can do for your country.

My fellow citizens of the world: Ask not what America will do for you, but what together we can do for the freedom of man.

Finally, whether you are citizens of America or citizens of the world, ask of us here the same high standards of strength and sacrifice which we ask of you. With a good conscience our only sure reward, with history the final judge of our deeds, let us go forth to lead the land we love, asking His blessing and His help, but knowing that here on earth God's work must truly be our own.

"I HAVE A DREAM"
Martin Luther King, Jr.

Five score years ago, a great American, in whose symbolic shadow we stand today, signed the Emancipation Proclamation. This momentous decree came as a great beacon of light of hope to millions of Negro slaves who had been seared in the flames of withering injustice. It came as a joyous daybreak to end the long night of their captivity.

But one hundred years later, the Negro still is not free. One hundred years later, the life of the Negro is still sadly crippled by the manacles of segregation and the chains of discrimination.

One hundred years later, the Negro lives on a lonely island of poverty in the midst of a vast ocean of material prosperity. One hundred years later, the Negro is still languished in the corners of American society and finds himself an exile in his own land. So we have come here today to dramatize a shameful condition.

In a sense we have come to our nation's capital to cash a check. When the architects of our republic wrote the magnificent words of the Constitution and the Declaration of Independence, they were signing a promissory note to which every American was to fall heir. This note was a promise that all men, yes, black men as well as white men, would be guaranteed the unalienable rights of life, liberty, and the pursuit of happiness.

It is obvious today that America has defaulted on this promissory note insofar as her citizens of color are concerned. Instead of honoring this sacred obligation, America has given the Negro people a bad check, which has come back marked "insufficient funds."

But we refuse to believe that the bank of justice is bankrupt. We refuse to believe that there are insufficient funds in the great vaults of opportunity of this nation. So we have come to cash this check — a check that will give us upon demand the riches of freedom and the security of justice.

We have also come to this hallowed spot to remind America of the fierce urgency of now. This is no time to engage in the luxury of cooling off or to take the tranquilizing drug of gradualism. Now is the time to make real the promises of democracy. Now is the time to rise from the dark and desolate valley of segregation to the sunlit path of racial justice. Now is the time to lift our nation from the quicksands of racial injustice to the solid rock of brotherhood. Now is the time to make justice a reality for all of God's children.

It would be fatal for the nation to overlook the urgency of the movement and to underestimate the determination of the Negro. This sweltering summer of the Negro's legitimate discontent will not pass until there is an invigorating autumn of freedom and equality. 1963 is not an end but a beginning. Those who hope that the Negro needed to blow off steam and will now be content will have a rude awakening if the nation returns to business as usual.

There will be neither rest nor tranquility in America until the Negro is granted his citizenship rights. The whirlwinds of revolt will continue to shake the foundations of our nation until the bright day of justice emerges.

But there is something that I must say to my people who stand on the warm threshold which leads into the palace of justice. In the process of gaining our rightful place we must not be guilty of wrongful deeds.

Let us not seek to satisfy our thrist for freedom by drinking from the cup of bitterness and hatred. We must forever conduct our struggle on the high place of dignity and discipline. We must not allow our creative protest to degenerate into physical violence. Again and again we must rise to the majestic heights of meeting physical force with soul force.

The marvelous new militancy which has engulfed the Negro community must not lead us to a distrust of all white people, for many of our white brothers, as evidenced by their presence here today, have come to realize that their destiny is tied up with our destiny and they have come to realize that their freedom is inextricably bound to our freedom. This offense we share mounted to storm the battlements of injustice must be carried forth by a bi-racial army. We cannot walk alone.

And as we walk, we must make the pledge that we shall always march ahead. We cannot turn back. There are those who are asking the devotees of civil rights, "When will you be satisfied?" We can never be satisfied as long as the Negro is the victim of the unspeakable horrors of police brutality.

We can never be satisfied as long as our bodies, heavy with the fatigue of travel, cannot gain lodging in the motels of the highways and hotels of the cities. We cannot be satisfied as long as the Negro's basic mobility is from a smaller ghetto to a larger one.

We can never be satisfied as long as our children are stripped of their selfhood and robbed of their dignity by signs stating "for whites only." We cannot be satisfied as long as a Negro in Mississippi cannot vote and a Negro in New York believes he has nothing for which to vote. No, we are not satisfied, and we will not be satisfied until justice rolls down like waters and righteousness like a mighty stream.

I am not unmindful that some of you have come here out of excessive trials and tribulation. Some of you have come fresh from narrow jail cells. Some of you have come from areas where your quest for freedom left you battered by the storms of persecution and staggered by the winds of police brutality. You have been the veterans of creative suffering. Continue to work with the faith that unearned suffering is redemptive.

Go back to Mississippi; go back to Alabama; go back to South Carolina; go back to Georgia; go back to the slums and ghettos of the Northern cities, knowing that somehow this situation can, and will be changed. Let us not wallow in the valley of despair.

So I say to you, my friends, that even though we must face the difficulties of today and tomorrow, I still have a dream. It is a dream deeply rooted in the American dream that one day this nation will rise up and live out the true meaning of its creed — we hold these truths to be self evident, that all men are created equal.

I have a dream that one day on the red hills of Georgia, sons of former slaves and sons of former slave-owners will be able to sit down together at the table of brotherhood.

I have a dream that one day, even the state of Mississippi, a state sweltering with the heat of injustice, sweltering with the heat of oppression will be transformed into an oasis of freedom and justice.

I have a dream my four little children will one day live in a nation where they will not be judged by the color of their skin but by the content of their character. I have a dream today!

I have a dream that one day, down in Alabama, with its vicious racists, with its governor having his lips dripping with the words of interposition and nullification, that one day, right there in Alabama, little black boys and black girls will be able to join hands with little white boys and white girls as sisters and brothers. I have a dream today!

I have a dream that one day every valley shall be exalted, every hill and mountain shall be made low, the rough places shall be made plain, and the crooked places shall be made straight and the glory of the Lord will be revealed and all flesh shall see it together.

This is our hope. This is the faith that I go back to the South with.

With this faith we will be able to hew out of the mountain of despair a stone of hope. With this faith we will be able to transform the jangling discords of our nation into a beautiful symphony of brotherhood.

With this faith we will be able to work together, to pray together, to struggle together, to go to jail together, to stand up for freedom together, knowing that we will be free one day. This will be the day when all of God's children will be able to sing with new meaning — "my country 'tis of thee, sweet land of liberty, of thee I sing; land where my fathers died, land of the pilgrim's pride; from every mountain side, let freedom ring" — and if America is to be a great nation, this must become true.

And so let freedom ring from the prodigious hilltops of New Hampshire.

Let freedom ring from the mighty mountains of New York.

Let freedom ring from the heightening Alleghenies of Pennsylvania.

Let freedom ring from the snow-capped Rockies of Colorado.

Let freedom ring from the curvaceous slopes of California. But not only that.

Let freedom ring from Stone Mountain of Georgia.

Let freedom ring from Lookout Mountain of Tennessee.

Let freedom ring from every hill and molehill of Mississippi, from every mountain side, let freedom ring.

And when this happens, and when we allow freedom to ring, when we let it ring from every village and hamlet, from every state and city, we will be able to speed up that day when all of God's children — black men and white men, Jews and Gentiles, Catholics and Protestants — will be able to join hands and to sing in the words of the old Negro spiritual, "Free at last, free at last; thank God Almighty, we are free at last."

FAREWELL ADDRESS TO CONGRESS
Douglas MacArthur

Mr. President, Mr. Speaker, and distinguished Members of the Congress, I stand on this rostrum with a sense of deep humility and great pride — humility in the wake of those great American architects of our history who have stood here before me, pride in the reflection that this forum of legislative debate represents human liberty in the purest form yet devised. Here are centered the hopes, and aspirations, and faith of the entire human race.

I do not stand here as advocate for any partisan cause, for the issues are fundamental and reach quite beyond the realm of partisan consideration. They must be resolved on the highest plane of national interest if our course is to prove sound and our future protected. I trust, therefore, that you will do me the justice of receiving that which I have to say as solely expressing the considered viewpoint of a fellow American. I address you with neither rancor nor bitterness in the fading twilight of life with but one purpose in mind — to serve my country.

The issues are global and so interlocked that to consider the problems of one sector, oblivious to those of another, is but to court disaster for the whole.

While Asia is commonly referred to as the gateway to Europe, it is no less true that Europe is the gateway to Asia, and the broad influence of the one cannot fail to have its impact upon the other.

There are those who claim our strength is inadequate to protect on both fronts — that we cannot divide our effort. I can think of no greater expression of defeatism. If a potential enemy can divide his strength on two fronts, it is for us to counter his effort.

The Communist threat is a global one. Its successful advance in one sector threatens the destruction of every other sector. You cannot appease or otherwise surrender to communism in Asia without simultaneously undermining our efforts to halt its advance in Europe.

Beyond pointing out these general truisms, I shall confine my discussion to the general areas of Asia. Before one may objectively assess the situation now existing there, he must comprehend something of Asia's past and the revolutionary changes which have marked her course up to the present. Long exploited by the so-called colonial powers, with little opportunity to achieve any degree of social justice, individual dignity, or a higher standard of life such as guided our own noble administration of the Philippines, the peoples of Asia found their opportunity in the war just past to throw off the shackles of colonialism, and now see the dawn of new opportunity, a heretofore unfelt dignity and the self-respect of political freedom.

Mustering half of the earth's population and 60 percent of its natural resources, these peoples are rapidly consolidating a new force, both moral and material, with which to raise the living standard and erect adaptations of the design of modern progress to their own distinct cultural environments. Whether one adheres to the concept of colonization or not, this is the direction of Asian progress and it may not be stopped. It is a corollary to the shift of the world economic frontiers, as the whole epicenter of world affairs rotates back toward the area whence it started. In this situation it becomes vital that our own country orient its policies in consonance with this basic evolutionary condition rather than pursue a course blind to the reality that the colonial era is now past and the Asian peoples covet the right to shape their own free destiny. What they seek now is friendly guidance, understanding, and support, not imperious direction; the dignity of equality, not the shame of subjugation. Their prewar standards of life, pitifully low, is infinitely lower now in the devastation left in war's wake. World ideologies play little part in Asian thinking and are little understood. What the peoples strive for is the opportunity for a little more food in their stomachs, a little better clothing on their backs, a little firmer roof over their heads, and the realization of the normal nationalist urge for political freedom. These political-social conditions have but an indirect bearing upon our own national security, but do form a backdrop to contemporary planning which must be thoughtfully considered if we are to avoid the pitfalls of unrealism.

Of more direct and immediate bearing upon our national security are the changes wrought in the strategic potential of the Pacific Ocean in the course of the past war. Prior thereto, the western strategic frontier of the United States lay on the littoral line of the Americas with an exposed island salient extending out through Hawaii, Midway, and Guam to the Philippines. That salient proved not an outpost of strength but an avenue of weakness along which the enemy could and did attack. The Pacific was a potential area of advance for any predatory force intent upon striking at the bordering land areas.

All this was changed by our Pacific victory. Our strategic frontier then shifted to embrace the entire Pacific Ocean which became a vast moat to protect us as long as we hold it. Indeed, it acts as a protective shield for all of the Americas and all free lands of the Pacific Ocean area. We control it to the shores of Asia by a chain of islands extending in an arc from the Aleutians to the Mariannas held by us and our free allies.

From this island chain we can dominate with sea and air power every Asiatic port from Vladivostok to Singapore and prevent any hostile movement into the Pacific. Any predatory attack from Asia must be an amphibious effort. No amphibious force can be successful without control of the sea lanes and the air over those lanes in its avenue of advance. With naval and air supremacy and modest ground elements to defend bases, any major attack from continental Asia toward us or our friends of the Pacific would be doomed to failure. Under such conditions the Pacific no longer represents menacing avenues of approach for a prospective invader — it assumes instead the friendly aspect of a peaceful lake. Our line of defense is a natural one and can be maintained with a minimum of military effort and expense. It envisions no attack against anyone nor does it provide the bastions essential for offensive operations, but properly maintained would be an invincible defense against aggression.

The holding of this littoral defense line in the western Pacific is entirely dependent upon holding all segments thereof, for any major breach of that line by an unfriendly power would render vulnerable to determined attack every other segment.

This is a military estimate as to which I have yet to find a military leader who will take exception.

For that reason I have strongly recommended in the past as a matter of military urgency that under no circumstances must Formosa fall under Communist control. Such an eventuality would at once threaten the freedom of the Philippines and the loss of Japan, and might well force our western frontier back to the coasts of California, Oregon, and Washington.

To understand the changes which now appear upon the Chinese mainland, one must understand the changes in Chinese character and culture over the past 50 years. China up to 50 years ago was completely nonhomogeneous, being compartmented into groups divided against each other. The warmaking tendency was almost nonexistent, as they still followed the tenets of the Confucian ideal of pacifist culture. At the turn of the century, under the regime of Chan So Lin, efforts toward greater homogeneity produced the start of a nationalist urge. This was further and more successfully developed under the leadership of Chiang Kai-shek but has been brought to its greatest fruition under the present regime, to the point that it has now taken on the character of a united nationalism of increasingly dominant aggressive tendencies. Through these past 50 years, the Chinese people have thus become militarized in their concepts and in their ideals. They now constitute excellent soldiers with competent staffs and commanders. This has produced a new and dominant power in Asia which for its own purpose is allied with Soviet Russia, but which in its own concepts and methods has become aggressively imperialistic with a lust for expansion and increased power normal to this type of imperialism. There is little of the ideological concept either one way or another in the Chinese make-up. The standard of living is so low and the capital accumulation has been so thoroughly dissipated by war that the masses are desperate and avid to follow any leadership which seems to promise the alleviation of local stringencies. I have from the beginning believed that the Chinese Communists' support of the North Koreans was the dominant one. Their interests are at present parallel to those of the Soviet, but I believe that the aggressiveness recently displayed not only in Korea, but also in Indochina and Tibet and pointing potentially toward the south, reflects predominantly the same lust for the expansion of power which has animated every would-be conqueror since the beginning of time.

The Japanese people since the war have undergone the greatest reformation recorded in modern history. With a commendable will, eagerness to learn, and marked capacity to understand, they have from the ashes left in war's wake, erected in Japan an edifice dedicated to the primacy of individual liberty and personal dignity, and in the ensuing process there has been created a truly representative government committed to the advance of political morality, freedom of economic enterprise and social justice. Politically, economically and socially Japan is now abreast of many free nations of the earth and will not again fail the universal trust. That it may be counted upon to wield a profoundly beneficial influence over the course of events in Asia is attested by the magnificent manner in which the Japanese people have met the recent challenge of war, unrest, and confusion surrounding them from the outside, and checked communism within their own frontiers without the slightest slackening in their forward progress. I sent all four of our occupation divisions to the Korean battle front without the slightest qualms as to the effect of the resulting power vacuum upon Japan. The results fully justified my faith. I know of no nation more serene, orderly, and industrious — nor in which higher hopes can be entertained for future constructive service in the advance of the human race.

Of our former wards, the Philippines, we can look forward in confidence that the existing unrest will be corrected and a strong and healthy nation will grow in the longer aftermath of war's terrible destructiveness. We must be patient and understanding and never fail them, as in our hour of need they did not fail us. A Christian nation, the Philippines stand as a mighty bulwark of Christianity in the Far East, and its capacity for high moral leadership in Asia is unlimited.

On Formosa, the Government of the Republic of China, has had the opportunity to refute by action much of the malicious gossip which so undermined the strength of its leadership on the Chinese mainland. The Formosa people are receiving a just and enlightened administration with majority representation on the organs of government; and politically, economically and socially they appear to be advancing along sound and constructive lines.

With this brief insight into the surrounding areas I now turn to the Korean conflict. While I was not consulted prior to the President's decision to intervene in support of the Republic of Korea, that decision, from a military standpoint, proved a sound one as we hurled back the invaders and decimated his forces. Our victory was complete and our objectives within reach when Red China intervened with numerically superior ground forces. This created a new war and an entirely new situation — a situation not contemplated when our forces were committed against the North Korean invaders — a situation which called for new decisions in the diplomatic sphere to permit the realistic adjustment of military strategy. Such decisions have not been forthcoming.

While no man in his right mind would advocate sending our ground forces into continental China and such was never given a thought, the new situation did urgently demand a drastic revision of strategic planning if our political aim was to defeat this new enemy as we had defeated the old.

Apart from the military need as I saw it to neutralize the sanctuary protection given the enemy north of the Yalu, I felt that military necessity in the conduct of the war made mandatory:

1. The intensification of our economic blockade against China;

2. The imposition of a naval blockade against the China coast;

3. Removal of restrictions on air reconnaissance of China's coast areas and of Manchuria;

4. Removal of restrictions on the forces of the Republic of China on Formosa with logistical support to contribute to their effective operations against the common enemy.

For entertaining these views, all professionally designed to support our forces committed to Korea and bring hostilities to an end with the least possible delay and at a saving of countless American and Allied lives, I have been severely criticized in lay circles, principally abroad, despite my understanding that from a military standpoint the above views have been fully shared in the past by practically every military leader concerned with the Korean campaign, including our own Joint Chiefs of Staff.

I called for reinforcements, but was informed that reinforcements were not available. I made clear that if not permitted to destroy the build-up bases north of the Yalu; if not permitted to utilize the friendly Chinese force of some 600,000 men on Formosa; if not permitted to blockade the China coast to prevent the Chinese Reds from getting succor from without; and if there were to be no hope of major reinforcements, the position of the command from the military standpoint forbade victory. We could not hold in Korea by constant maneuver and at an approximate area where our supply line advantages were in balance with the supply line disadvantages of the enemy, but we could hope at best for only an indecisive campaign, with its terrible and constant attrition upon our forces if the enemy utilized his full military potential. I have constantly called for the new political decisions essential to a solution. Efforts have been made to distort my position. It has been said, in effect, that I am a warmonger. Nothing could be further from the truth. I know war as few other men now living know it, and nothing to me is more revolting. I have long advocated its complete abolition as its very destructiveness on both friend and foe has rendered it useless as a means of settling international disputes. Indeed, on the 2nd of September 1945, just following the surrender of the Japanese Nation on the battleship Missouri, I formally cautioned as follows:

Men since the beginning of time have sought peace. Various methods through the ages have been attempted to devise an international process to prevent or settle disputes between nations. From the very start, workable methods were found insofar as individual citizens were concerned, but the mechanics of an instrumentality of larger international scope have never been successful. Military alliances, balances of power, leagues of nations, all in turn failed, leaving the only path to be by way of the crucible of war. The utter destructiveness of war now blots out this alternative. We have had our last chance. If we will not devise some greater and more equitable system, Armageddon will be at our door. The problem basically is theological and involves a spiritual recrudescence and improvement of human character that will synchronize with our almost matchless advances in science, art, literature, and all material and cultural developments of the past 2,000 years. It must be of the spirit if we are to save the flesh.

But once war is forced upon us, there is no other alternative than to apply every available means to bring it to a swift end. War's very object is victory — not prolonged indecision. In war, indeed, there can be no substitute for victory. There are some who for varying reasons would appease Red China. They are blind to history's clear lessons. For history teaches with unmistakable emphasis that appeasement but begets new and bloodier war. It points to no single instance where the end has justified that means — where appeasement has led to more than a sham peace. Like blackmail, it lays the basis for new and successively greater demands, until, as in blackmail, violence becomes the only other alternative. Why, my soldiers asked of me, surrender military advantages to an enemy in the field? I could not answer. Some may say to avoid spread of the conflict into an all-out war with China; others, to avoid Soviet intervention. Neither explanation seems valid. For China is already engaging with the maximum power it can commit and the Soviet will not necessarily mesh its actions with our moves. Like a cobra, any new enemy will more likely strike whenever it feels that the relativity in military or other potential is in its favor on a world-wide basis.

The tragedy of Korea is further heightened by the fact that as military action is confined to its territorial limits, it condemns that nation, which it is our purpose to save, to suffer the devastating impact of full naval and air bombardment, while the enemy's sanctuaries are fully protected from such attack and devastation. Of the nations of the world, Korea alone, up to now, is the sole one which has risked its all against communism. The magnificence of the courage and fortitude of the Korean people defies description. They have chosen to risk death rather than slavery. Their last words to me were "Don't scuttle the Pacific."

I have just left your fighting sons in Korea. They have met all tests there and I can report to you without reservation they are splendid in every way. It was my constant effort to preserve them and end this savage conflict honorably and with the least loss of time and a minimum sacrifice of life. Its growing bloodshed has caused me the deepest anguish and anxiety. Those gallant men will remain often in my thoughts and in my prayers always.

I am closing my 52 years of military service. When I joined the Army even before the turn of the century, it was the fulfillment of all my boyish hopes and dreams. The world has turned over many times since I took the oath on the plain at West Point, and the hopes and dreams have long since vanished. But I still remember the refrain of one of the most popular barrack ballads of that day which proclaimed most proudly that — "Old soldiers never die; they just fade away."

And like the old soldier of that ballad, I now close my military career and just fade away — an old soldier who tried to do his duty as God gave him the light to see that duty.

Good-by.

CLOSING ADDRESS TO THE 1934 NAZI CONGRESS IN NUREMBERG:
Adolph Hitler

The Sixth Party Rally is coming to an end. What millions of Germans outside our ranks may simply have rated as an imposing display of political power was infinitely more for hundreds of thousands of fighters; the great personal, political and spiritual meeting of the old fighters and battle comrades. And perhaps, in spite of the spectacular forcefulness of this imposing review of the armies of the Party, many among them were wistfully thinking back to the days when it was difficult to be a National Socialist. For when our Party comprised just seven people, it already formulated two principles: it wanted to be a truly ideological party; it wanted, uncompromisingly, sole and absolute power in Germany.

We, as a party, had to remain a minority, because we mobilized the most valuable elements of fight and sacrifice in the nation, and they are never a majority but always a minority. And since this best racial component of the German nation, proudly self-assured, courageously, and daringly, demanded leadership of the Reich and the people, the people followed its leadership in ever greater numbers and subordinated themselves to it.

The German people are happily aware that the eternal flight of appearances has now been replaced by one stable pole, which sensing and knowing that it represented the very best German blood, rose to the leadership of the nation and is determined to keep this leadership, and exercise it, and never give it up again. There will always be only one segment of a people who will be really active fighters, and more is demanded of them than of the millions of other people. For them it is not enough to simply say, "I believe;" they take an oath, "I shall fight."

The Party will for all times be the leadership reservoir of the German people, unchangeable in its teachings, hard as steel in its organization, pliable and adaptable in its tactics, and in its total appearance the manifestation of the spirit of the nation. Again it must be that all decent Germans become National Socialists. Only the best National Socialists become party members.

Formerly, our opponents saw to it that through prohibition and persecution our movement was periodically purged of the light chaff that began to settle in it. Now we must practice selectiveness ourselves and expel what has proved to be rotten and therefore not of our kind. It is our wish and intent that this state and this Reich shall endure through the millenia ahead. We can rejoice in the knowledge that the future belongs totally to us.

Where the older generations might still waver, the youth is sworn to us and given to us, body and soul. Only if we realize in the Party the ultimate essence and idea of National Socialism, through the joint effort of all of us, will it forever and indestructibly be a possession of the German people and the German nation. Then the splendid and glorious army of the old and proud armed services of our nation will be joined by the no less tradition-bound leadership of the party and together these two establishments will form and firm the German people and carry on their shoulders the German state and German Reich.

At this hour, tens of thousands of party comrades are beginning to leave town. While some are still reminiscing, others are getting ready for the next roll call, and always people will come and go, and always they will be gripped anew, gladdened, and inspired, for the idea and the Movement are expressions of the life of our people and therefore, symbols of eternity.

Long live the National Socialist Movement.

Long live Germany!

RUDOLPH HESS:

The party is Hitler! Hitler is Germany as Germany is Hitler!

1942 STATE-OF-THE-UNION ADDRESS:
Franklin D. Roosevelt

In fulfilling my duty to report upon the State of the Union, I am proud to say to you that the spirit of the American people was never higher than it is today — the Union was never more closely knit together — this country was never more deeply determined to face the solemn tasks before it.

The response of the American people has been instantaneous, and it will be sustained until our security is assured.

Exactly one year ago today I said to the Congress: "When the dictators . . . are ready to make war upon us, they will not wait for an act of war on our part . . . They — not we — will choose the time and the place and the method of their attack."

We now know their choice of the time: a peaceful Sunday morning — December 7, 1941.

We know their choice of the place: an American outpost in the Pacific.

We know their choice of the method: the method of Hitler himself.

Japan's scheme of conquest goes back half a century. It was not merely a policy of seeking living room: it was a plan which included the subjugation of all the peoples in the Far East and in the islands of the Pacific, and the domination of that ocean by Japanese military and naval control of the western coasts of North, Central, and South America.

The development of this ambitious conspiracy was marked by the war against China in 1894; the subsequent occupation of Korea; the war against Russia in 1904; the illegal fortification of the mandated Pacific islands following 1920; the seizure of Manchuria in 1931; and the invasion of China in 1937.

A similar policy of criminal conquest was adopted by Italy. The Fascists first revealed their imperial designs in Libya and Tripoli. In 1935 they seized Abyssinia. Their goal was the domination of all North Africa, Egypt, parts of France, and the entire Mediterranean world.

But the dreams of empire of the Japanese and Fascist leaders were modest in comparison with the gargantuan aspirations of Hitler and his Nazis. Even before they came to power in 1933, their plans for that conquest had been drawn. Those plans provided for ultimate domination, not of any one section of the world, but of the whole earth and all oceans on it.

When Hitler organized his Berlin-Rome-Tokyo alliance, all these plans of conquest became a single plan. Under this, in addition to her own schemes of conquest, Japan's role was obviously to cut off our supply of weapons to Britain, and Russia and China — weapons which increasingly were speeding the day of Hitler's doom. The act of Japan at Pearl Harbor was intended to stun us — to terrify us to such an extent that we would divert our industrial and military strength to the Pacific area, or even to our continental defense.

The plan has failed in its purpose. We have not been stunned. We have not been terrified or confused. This very reassembling of the Seventy-seventh Congress today is proof of that; for the mood of quiet, grim resolution which here prevails bodes ill for those who conspired and collaborated to murder world peace.

That mood is stronger than any mere desire for revenge. It expresses the will of the American people to make very certain that the world will never so suffer again.

Admittedly, we have been faced with hard choices. It was bitter, for example, not to be able to relieve the heroic and historic defenders of Wake Island. It was bitter for us not to be able to land a million men in a thousand ships in the Philippine Islands.

But this adds only to our determination to see to it that the Stars and Stripes will fly again over Wake and Guam. Yes, see to it that the brave people of the Philippines will be rid of Japanese imperialism; and will live in freedom, security, and independence.

Powerful and offensive actions must and will be taken in proper time. The consolidation of the United Nations' total war effort against our common enemies is being achieved.

That was and is the purpose of the conferences which have been held during the past two weeks in Washington, and

Moscow and Chungking. That is the primary objective of the declaration of solidarity signed in Washington on January 1, 1942, by 26 nations united against the Axis powers.

Difficult choices may have to be made in the months to come. We do not shrink from such decisions. We and those united with us will make those decisions with courage and determination.

Plans have been laid here and in the other capitals for coordinated and cooperative action by all the United Nations — military action and economic action. Already we have established, as you know, unified command of land, sea, and air forces in the southwestern Pacific theater of war. There will be a continuation of conferences and consultations among military staffs, so that the plans and operations of each will fit into the general strategy designed to crush the enemy. We shall not fight isolated wars — each Nation going its own way. These 26 nations are united — not in spirit and determination alone, but in the broad conduct of the war in all its phases.

For the first time since the Japanese and the Fascists and the Nazis started along their blood-stained course of conquest they now face the fact that superior forces are assembling against them. Gone forever are the days when the aggressors could attack and destroy their victims one by one without unity of resistance. We of the United Nations will so dispose our forces that we can strike at the common enemy wherever the greatest damage can be done him.

The militarists of Berlin and Tokyo started this war. But the massed, angered forces of common humanity will finish it.

Destruction of the material and spiritual centers of civilization — this has been and still is the purpose of Hitler and his Italian and Japanese chessmen. They would wreck the power of the British Commonwealth and Russia and China and the Netherlands — and then combine all their forces to achieve their ultimate goal, the conquest of the United States.

They know that victory for us means victory for freedom.

They know that victory for us means victory for the institution of democracy — the ideal of the family, the simple principles of common decency and humanity.

They know that victory for us means victory for religion.

And they could not tolerate that. The world is too small to

provide adequate "living room" for both Hitler and God. In proof of that, the Nazis have now announced their plan for enforcing their new German, pagan religion all over the world — a plan by which the Holy Bible and Cross of Mercy would be displaced by Mein Kampf and the swastika and the naked sword.

Our own objectives are clear; the objective of smashing the militarism imposed by war lords upon their enslaved peoples — the objective of liberating the subjugated Nations — the objective of establishing and securing freedom of religion, freedom from want, and freedom from fear everywhere in the world.

We shall not stop short of these objectives — nor shall we be satisfied merely to gain them and then call it a day. I know that I speak for the American people — and I have good reason to believe that I speak also for all the other people who fight with us — when I say that this time we are determined not only to win the war, but also to maintain the security of the peace that will follow.

But we know that modern methods of warfare make it a task, not only of shooting and fighting, but an even more urgent one of working and producing.

Victory requires the actual weapons of war and the means of transporting them to a dozen points of combat.

It will not be sufficient for us and the other United Nations to produce a slightly superior supply of munitions to that of Germany, Japan, Italy, and the stolen industries in the countries which they have overrun.

The superiority of the United Nations in munitions and ships must be overwhelming — so overwhelming that the Axis can never hope to catch up with it. And so, in order to attain this overwhelming superiority the United States must build planes and tanks and guns and ships to the utmost limit of our national capacity. We have the ability and capacity to produce arms not only for our own forces, but also for the armies, navies, and air forces fighting on our side.

And our overwhelming superiority of armament must be adequate to put weapons of war at the proper time into the hands of those men in the conquered Nations who stand ready to seize the first opportunity to revolt against their

German and Japanese oppressors, and against the traitors in their own ranks, known by the already infamous name of "Quislings." And I think that it is a fair prophecy to say that, as we get guns to the patriots in those lands, they too will fire shots heard 'round the world.

This production of ours in the United States must be raised far above present levels, even though it will mean the dislocation of the lives and occupations of millions of our own people. We must raise our sights all along the production line. Let no man say it cannot be done. It must be done — and we have undertaken to do it.

I have just sent a letter of directive to the appropriate departments and agencies of our Government, ordering that immediate steps be taken:

First, to increase our production rate of airplanes so rapidly that in this year, 1942, we shall produce 60,000 planes, 10,000 more than the goal that we set a year and a half ago. This includes 45,000 combat planes — bombers, dive bombers, pursuit planes. The rate of increase will be maintained and continued so that next year, 1943, we shall produce 125,000 airplanes, including 100,000 combat planes.

Second, to increase our production rate of tanks so rapidly that in this year, 1942, we shall produce 45,000 tanks; and to continue that increase so that next year, 1943, we shall produce 75,000 tanks.

Third, to increase our production rate of anti-aircraft guns so rapidly that in this year, 1942, we shall produce 20,000 of them; and continue that increase so that next year, 1943, we shall produce 35,000 anti-aircraft guns.

And fourth, to increase our production rate of merchant ships so rapidly that in this year, 1942, we shall build 6,000,000 dead-weight tons as compared with a 1941 completed production of 1,100,000. And finally, we shall continue that increase so that next year, 1943, we shall build 10,000,000 tons of shipping.

These figures and similar figures for a multitude of other implements of war will give the Japanese and the Nazis a little idea of just what they accomplished in the attack at Pearl Harbor.

And I rather hope that all these figures which I have given

will become common knowledge in Germany and Japan.

Our task is hard — our task is unprecedented — and the time is short. We must strain every existing armament-producing facility to the utmost. We must convert every available plant and tool to war production. That goes all the way from the greatest plants to the smallest — from the huge automobile industry to the village machine shop.

Production for war is based on men and women — the human hands and brains which collectively we call Labor. Our workers stand ready to work long hours; to turn out more in a day's work; to keep the wheels turning and the fires burning twenty-four hours a day, and seven days a week. They realize well that on the speed and efficiency of their work depend the lives of their sons and their brothers on the fighting fronts.

Production for war is based on metals and raw materials — steel, copper, rubber, aluminum, zinc, tin. Greater and greater quantities of them will have to be diverted to war purposes. Civilian use of them will have to be cut further and still further — and, in many cases, completely eliminated.

War costs money. So far, we have hardly begun to pay for it. We have devoted only 15 percent of our national income to national defense. As will appear in my Budget Message tomorrow, our war program for the coming fiscal year will cost 56 billion dollars or, in other words, more than half of the estimated annual national income. That means taxes and bonds and bonds and taxes. It means cutting luxuries and other non-essentials. In a word, it means an "all-out" war by individual effort and family effort in a united country.

Only this all-out scale of production will hasten the ultimate all-out victory. Speed will count. Lost ground can always be regained — lost time never. Speed will save lives; speed will save this Nation which is in peril; speed will save our freedom and our civilization — and slowness has never been an American characteristic.

As the United States goes into its full stride, we must always be on guard against misconceptions which will arise, some of them naturally, or which will be planted among us by our enemies.

We must guard against complacency. We must not underrate the enemy. He is powerful and cunning — and cruel and ruthless. He will stop at nothing that gives him a chance to kill and to destroy. He has trained his people to believe that their hightest perfection is achieved by waging war. For many years he has prepared for this very conflict — planning, and plotting, and training, arming, and fighting. We have already tasted defeat. We may suffer further setbacks. We must face the fact of a hard war, a long war, a bloody war, a costly war.

We must, on the other hand, guard against defeatism. That has been one of the chief weapons of Hitler's propaganda machine — used time and again with deadly results. It will not be used successfully on the American people.

We must guard against divisions among ourselves and among all other United Nations. We must be particularly vigilant against racial discrimination in any of its ugly forms. Hitler will try again to breed mistrust and suspicion between one individual and another, one group and another, one race and another, one Government and another. He will try to use the same technique of falsehood and rumor-mongering with which he divided France from Britain. He is trying to do this even now. But he will find a unity of will and purpose against him, which will persevere until the destruction of all his black designs upon the freedom and safety of the people of the world.

We cannot wage this war in a defensive spirit. As our power and our resources are fully mobilized, we shall carry the attack against the enemy — we shall hit him and hit him again wherever and whenever we can reach him.

We must keep him far from our shores, for we intend to bring this battle to him on his own home grounds.

American armed forces must be used at any place in all the world where it seems advisable to engage the forces of the enemy. In some cases these operations will be defensive, in order to protect key positions. In other cases, these operations will be offensive, in order to strike at the common enemy, with a view to his complete encirclement and eventual total defeat.

American armed forces will operate at many points in the Far East.

American armed forces will be on all the oceans — helping to guard the essential communications which are vital to the

United Nations.

American land and air and sea forces will take stations in the British Isles — which constitute an essential fortress in this great world struggle.

American armed forces will help to protect this hemisphere — and also help to protect bases outside this hemisphere, which could be used for an attack on the Americas.

If any of our enemies, from Europe or from Asia, attempt long-range raids by "suicide" squadrons of bombing planes, they will do so only in the hope of terrorizing our people and disrupting our morale. Our people are not afraid of that. We know that we may have to pay a heavy price for freedom. We will pay this price with a will. Whatever the price, it is a thousand times worth it. No matter what our enemies, in their desperation, may attempt to do to us — we will say, as the people of London have said, "We can take it." And what's more we can give it back — and we will give it back — with compound interest.

When our enemies challenged our country to stand up and fight, they challenged each and every one of us. And each and every one of us has accepted the challenge — for himself and for his Nation.

There were only some 400 United States Marines who in the heroic and historic defense of Wake Island inflicted such great losses on the enemy. Some of those men were killed in action; and others are now prisoners of war. When the survivors of that great fight are liberated and restored to their homes, they will learn that a hundred and thirty million of their fellow citizens have been inspired to render their own full share of service and sacrifice.

We can well say that our men on the fighting fronts have already proved that Americans today are just as rugged and just as tough as any of the heroes whose exploits we celebrate on the Fourth of July.

Many people ask, "When will this war end?" There is only one answer to that. It will end just as soon as we make it end, by our combined efforts, our combined strength, our combined determination to fight through and work through until the end — the end of militarism in Germany and Italy and Japan. Most certainly we shall not settle for less.

This is the spirit in which discussions have been conducted during the visit of the British Prime Minister to Washington. Mr. Churchill and I understand each other, our motives and our purposes. Together, during the past two weeks, we have faced squarely the major military and economic problems of this greatest world war.

All in our Nation have been cheered by Mr. Churchill's visit. We have been deeply stirred by his great message to us. He is welcome in our midst, and we unite in wishing him a safe return to his home.

For we are fighting on the same side with the British people, who fought alone for long, terrible months, and withstood the enemy with fortitude and tenacity and skill.

We are fighting on the same side with the Russian people who have seen the Nazi hordes swarm up to the very gates of Moscow, and who with almost superhuman will and courage have forced the invaders back into retreat.

We are fighting on the same side as the brave people of China — those millions who for four and a half long years have withstood bombs and starvation and have whipped the invaders time and again in spite of the superior Japanese equipment and arms.

Yes, we are fighting on the same side as the indomitable Dutch.

We are fighting on the same side as all the other Governments in exile, whom Hitler and all his armies and all his Gestapo have not been able to conquer.

But we of the United Nations are not making all this sacrifice of human effort and human lives to return to the kind of world we had after the last world war.

We are fighting today for security, for progress, and for peace, not only for outselves but for all men, not only for one generation but for all generations. We are fighting to cleanse the world of ancient evils, ancient ills.

Our enemies are guided by brutal cynicism, by unholy contempt for the human race. We are inspired by a faith that goes back through all the years to the first chapter of the Book of Genesis: "God created man in His own image."

We on our side are striving to be true to that divine heritage. We are fighting, as our fathers have fought, to uphold the doctrine that all men are equal in the sight of God. Those on the other side are striving to destroy this deep belief and to create a world in their own image — a world of tyranny and cruelty and serfdom.

That is the conflict that day and night now pervades our lives. No compromise can end that conflict. There never has been — there never can be — successful compromise between good and evil. Only total victory can reward the champions of tolerance, and decency, and freedom, and faith.